20⁰⁰
4/5

LABOR EMBATTLED

DAVID BRODY

Labor Embattled

HISTORY, POWER, RIGHTS

UNIVERSITY OF ILLINOIS PRESS

URBANA AND CHICAGO

1 2 3 4 5 C P 5 4 3 2 1

Library of Congress Cataloging-in-Publication Data
Brody, David, 1930–
Labor embattled : history, power, rights / David Brody.
p.   cm. — (The working class in American history)
Includes index.
ISBN 0-252-03004-4 (cloth : alk. paper)
ISBN 0-252-07246-4 (pbk. : alk. paper)
1. Labor movement—United States. 2. Labor unions—
United States. 3. Labor laws and legislation—United
States. I. Title. II. Series.
HD8066.B75   2005
331.88'0973—dc22   2004024022

Contents

Preface

The best way to explain what this book is about might be to start at the end, with a question of language. In the final essay I say that the National Labor Relations Act has been *hijacked* by its natural enemies. Hijack is an ugly word—slang, my outdated dictionary says—and not normally in an academic's vocabulary. I choose it because I do not want to disguise my dismay at the subversion of a great New Deal law. In this, I do not fault employers or their minions any more than I would the beasts of the field. Business is business. But how was the deed done? What in the American fabric of ideology, jurisprudence, and politics enabled a law intended to liberate workers to be transformed into a law that oppresses them? Questions like these spring from the troubled present, but the answers require a reading of the past. The premise of this book is that, in hard times, the historian's responsibility is to undertake that reading in hopes of being of assistance and even, if he or she sees a way, of suggesting a course of action.

Times of trouble, remarked the great historian Richard Hofstadter in 1968—a true time of American troubles—ignite the age-old tension between objectivity and engagement. Historians find themselves "caught between their desire to count in the world and their desire to understand it. . . . Their passion for understanding points back to the old interest in detachment," while a sense of urgency "plays upon their pragmatic impulse, their desire to get out of history some lessons that will be of use to the world." A historian of generous spirit, Hofstadter was sympathetic to both impulses. But he had just finished his book, *The Progressive Historians*, and found Turner, Beard, and Parrington wanting precisely on grounds of their political engagement. Hofstadter conceded that "this present-mindedness, though it has been responsible for major errors, has often brought with it a major access of new insight—bearing error and distortion not in arbitrary solitude but in a kind of illicit union with intellectual discovery." The very greatest talents, like Henry Adams or Tocqueville, somehow "produced from the inner tensions of their minds an equipoise that enable[d] them to superimpose upon their commitment a measure of detachment about the past." For lesser mortals, the bar seemed too high. The historian driven by the present is likely to fall into the discipline's "cardinal sin": "He may lose his respect for the integrity, the independence, the pastness, of the past."

In this book I want to take up Hofstadter's challenge. The sense of urgency to which he alluded is very much mine as I observe the calamity—decent jobs disappearing, income disparities widening, and diminishing collective power—that in recent years has overtaken the working people and institutions whose past I have long studied. Perhaps because I am of a later generation, I am also aware of a distinction that Hofstadter bypasses. Not all aspects of the past make equal claims on our sympathies. It would be grotesque, for example, for a historian of slavery to be neutral about slavery and unreasonable to expect detachment from a historian, say, of McCarthyism, or women's rights, or the environment. Labor history belongs in this circle. The current assault on workers' rights especially calls out for historical scrutiny. We have to make sense of the perversion of principle that goes by the name "a union-free environment," and that, in its corrosive effects, best explains why the vast majority of American workers in the private sector currently are defenseless against management's arbitrary powers. If I were persuaded by Hofstadter's fear of a lost respect for the "pastness" of the past, that would stop me. I am, however, more drawn by his suggestion that present-minded history can yield its own insights into the past. So that's the historian's reason for this book. I want to test Hofstadter's propositions. My essays are offered in this spirit of inquiry, for the reader to judge.

Book-writing historians normally aim at erasing the footprints of intellectual composition and—depending on their skill—presenting the reader with a finished, seamless work. This rule of the historian's craft doesn't apply to an enterprise like mine. I want the reader to see the footprints, even where the tracks wind dustily back to historiography. The opening essay is indeed of that sort, addressed to my fellow practitioners and rallying them on the basis of an exploration of the traditions of our field to what I call "applied labor history." The succeeding entries are, in effect, my own response to that appeal. They fall naturally into three groups. Chapters 2 and 3 might be considered introductory, the first an initial foray into applied labor history, followed by a much earlier essay exploring the institutional influences bearing on the expansion and contraction of the labor movement. The second group, chapters 4, 5, and 6, is about the battle over workplace reform that sprang up in the early Clinton years. The entries are varied, including reviews, a paper before an international audience, and two historical essays. The opening one, a contribution to the debate at its onset, explores the New Deal origins of the outlawing of shop committees. It is followed by a more academic article (chapter 5) taking up a question arising from that New Deal essay, with results that I think exemplify the stimulating effects of engaged history. What that essay reveals about "representatives of their own choosing" is in turn a link to the final chapters, which deal with labor rights and, as I put it in the opening entry, "the paradox that a labor law democratic on its face is also a bad law for workers." In contending with this paradox I found myself moving in contrary directions—into a historian's exploration of the abiding tension between freedom and solidarity in the American law of labor and, on that basis, into the realm of prescriptive argument in the final entries—this despite my opinion, along with Richard Hofstadter—that policy is not the business of historians. Readers of chapters 8 and 9 will, I hope, understand the reasoning that overcame my scruples.

My intention to offer these essays exactly as they had originally appeared, however, did not quite work out. Writing at different occasions and for varied audiences, I sometimes found it necessary to repeat arguments I had made elsewhere, but with the essays now side by side readers don't need those assists, so as best I could I have scrubbed the essays of repetition. To varying degrees I have also edited out contemporary references that proved of only passing importance or needlessly dated the essays. And where I found a better way of expressing myself, I succumbed to that temptation as well. So readers are forewarned that the plan of this book has been compromised. The tracks of my journey are there, but they have been doctored.

More than the normal complement of friends and critics have had a hand in this enterprise. In the case of chapter 8, an audience of scholars and fellow essay-writers discussed a preliminary version at a formal conference. Other essays were first delivered as papers or talks, always evoking stimulating comments and exchanges. And I was shameless about buttonholing colleagues and passersby when my ideas were percolating. There is no way of rendering an accurate accounting of credit due these inadvertent participants in my project except by a heartfelt expression of general thanks. I also thank Eric Arnesen, Dorothy Sue Cobble, Lizabeth Cohen, Melvyn Dubofsky, Alice Kessler-Harris, Daniel J. Leab, and Nelson Lichtenstein, all of whom responded generously to the University of Illinois Press's request for comments about my proposal for a collection of essays. Their thoughtful suggestions—although none specifically proposed the final form of this book—prompted me to rethink my original conception of a historiographically focused collection. Sue Cobble also read the submitted manuscript for the Press. Her searching comments are the main reason why, as indicated above, the essays are more heavily edited than I had originally intended; the book, I expect, is much the better for it. The second reader, David Montgomery, offered a generous evaluation and in addition wrote an acute commentary—as usual—for the issue of *New Labor Forum* in which the final entry appeared. Thanks are due, finally, to several editors—Mark Levinson at *Dissent*, Paula Finn at *New Labor Forum*, Stephen Wood at the *British Journal of Industrial Relations*, and Stanley Engerman, editor of the volume in which I first published chapter 8—and to all the publications that generously granted permission to reprint copyrighted materials. Credits are at the beginning of each essay.

The book is dedicated to Roland Marchand, an admired colleague who died too soon.

LABOR EMBATTLED

1   *Responsibilities of the Labor Historian*

Doing history is at once a solitary occupation and richly communal. Historians are like schools of fish, finely attuned to and glad of one another's company. Yet the historical "schools" they join are inherently unstable. Modes of interpretation form. They flourish. They break down. In the late 1980s breakdown was the impending stage of the "new" labor history—the dominant school at the time. The usual debate over what had gone wrong was more than usually intense, mainly, I think, because many of its adherents were so heavily invested in the new labor history. My part in the debate, however, was decidedly retrograde. I argued that a place to look for guidance was the scholarship against which the new labor historians had rebelled—the "old" labor history that went back to John R. Commons and the institutional economists of the Wisconsin School. Out of that argument came the following essay, first read in 1992 and published in 1993 under the title "Reconciling the Old Labor History and the New." The title reflects the essay's pedigree as an intervention in an historiographical debate. But its value for this volume is where I came out, hence a new title: "Responsibilities of the Labor Historian."

This essay originally appeared as "Reconciling the Old Labor History and the New," *Pacific Historical Review* 62 (Feb. 1993): 1–18. Copyright © 1993 by the Pacific Coast Branch, American Historical Association. Reprinted with permission.

On March 9, 1990, a crowd of labor historians gathered on the campus of the University of Wisconsin for a conference on the theme "The Wisconsin School and Beyond." Only an old-timer in the field would have fully savored the significance of this event, for Madison was the site of the "old" labor history. It was here that John R. Commons had settled in 1904, amassed the first great archives of labor records, and on that basis launched what still stands as the fundamental work in the field—the four-volume *History of Labor in the United States* (1918–35). It was here that one of Commons's former students, Selig Perlman, wrote *A Theory of the Labor Movement* (1928) and that Philip Taft, the foremost labor historian of the next generation, was trained. And, with adherents of the Commons school firmly entrenched in the economics department, the University of Wisconsin resisted the new wave of labor scholarship that transformed the field from the 1960s onward until, in that respect, it became isolated and stood virtually alone among major universities.

The conveners manifestly intended the conference to be a bridge-building exercise. Indeed, surveying the audience, the history chair at Wisconsin, John Milton Cooper, commented on the number of accomplished scholars sitting before him whom his department had considered at one time or another but had never been able to hire. In that spirit I gave a keynote talk exploring the ground that we all shared and argued for the continuing—no, increasing—relevance of the old labor history. The audience seemed on the whole unimpressed. What was the point of raking up the past? That was the view, for example, of one critic, who afterward wrote that the Wisconsin conference failed "to create an opportunity to engage on a critical level the current historiographical and theoretical controversies labor historians face."[1] I take his point. The unity of perspective that originally characterized the new labor history clearly has broken down. Anyone who follows the debates among labor historians must be struck by the cacophony of prescriptions for how the field should move.[2] But, far from registering impatience, I would submit that at just such a juncture we are in need of a longer view about where we came from.

My starting point is a paper I delivered in 1978 at the Organization of American Historians, "The Old Labor History and the New." As best I can recall, the title was not my idea but Eric Foner's, suggested to me on the phone by way of describing the kind of historiographical discussion the program committee had in mind—so that, clearly, there was nothing original about the notion; it was already very much in the air.[3] For anyone remembering the indifferent treatment of labor history at past conventions, the scene must have seemed truly remarkable. It was a single-paper session, filling the ballroom to capacity and crackling with excitement. What all this reflected, of course, was not anything I had to say but the felt need of an emerging generation of labor historians—the hall was packed with graduate students and fresh Ph.D.s—to get their bearings at the point when their field was about to take off. The old/new distinction did the trick for them. The "new" referred to the work of Herbert G. Gutman and David Montgomery—in particular, to their recent guidepost essays, respectively, "Work, Culture and Society in Industrializing America" (1973) and "Workers' Control of Machine Production in the Nineteenth Century" (1976)—and of younger scholars like Daniel Walkowitz, whose *Worker City, Company Town* (1978) just then launched what was to become the bellwether publication in the field, the University of Illinois Press's Working Class in American History Series.[4] The "old," of course, was the Wisconsin School of labor history. My paper, in fact, opened with a discussion of the Wisconsin School that concluded on this dismissive note: "So the labor economists, for all that they contributed to our knowledge of the labor movement, left us otherwise nearly ignorant of the history of the American worker."[5]

The new labor historians were never actually as hard on the Wisconsin School as my words might suggest. Gutman himself remarked in his 1973 essay that "much of value remains to be learned from the older labor historians," and that was I think a common (if mostly implicit) view. A few, who felt especially beholden for groundwork previously laid, were more forthright. This was true, for example, of Alexander Saxton, who at the start of his *Indispensable Enemy: Labor and the Anti-Chinese Movement in California* (1971) devoted a long, appreciative paragraph to Ira Cross, who had studied under Commons at Wisconsin. Cross and his Berkeley students, Saxton remarked, had done for Western labor history what the Madison group had achieved for labor's national history: provided the major narrative texts and created the archival basis for future work. Cross might not agree with much of his interpretation, Saxton conceded. "Nonetheless I have traveled in his company for many miles which I could scarcely have got through otherwise."[6]

As for me, I had my own reasons for seeing the Wisconsin School sympathetically. The last thing I had done prior to "The Old Labor History and the New" was an essay about Philip Taft. Taft had died in 1976 and, for a commemorative issue, *Labor History* asked me to write a critical assessment of his work. It wasn't a job I especially relished—I didn't think much of his AFL books (which was mostly what I knew), and the few times our paths had crossed I had never gotten a kind word out of him—but there was no way of saying no. So I sat down and read or re-

read Taft—not only the major books but also volume four of the Commons's *History,* which he had mostly written, the labor relations and policy writings, the IWW essays, and his rather critical handling of his mentor Selig Perlman. He was a much bigger character than I had thought, not only because of his fierce intellectual integrity and remarkable scholarly industry, or because of the working-class roots that had always informed his work, but also because he revealed in his dogged empiricism what must always have been the core strength of the Wisconsin School. "In [Taft]," I wrote with some feeling, "a new scholarly generation received the uncommon opportunity of beholding the personification of an earlier tradition in its full intellectual vigor."[7]

So then I went on and slammed that "earlier tradition" in my OAH paper. Why I did that seems in retrospect reasonably obvious: The new labor history needed something against which to define itself. The truth is that the old labor history was never really displaced. Its themes— unions, politics, strikes, and leadership—continued to dominate the articles published by *Labor History,* for example, and crept into even the most advanced of the new texts. That continuity was indeed what most respondents emphasized in answering the programmatic piece by Howard Kimeldorf that called for "Bringing the Unions Back In (or Why We Need a New Old Labor History)."[8] For his part, Kimeldorf made his target what he called "the tyranny of culturalism" so that, in its turn, the new labor history (or a main part of it) takes on a defining function as negative reference point for one of the next challenges. We should, I submit, read this redefining process—in its current as well as past incarnations—not as an expression of mean-spiritedness but as a means of clarifying the specific points of departure of fresh scholarship from what is already in place. Certainly that is the most useful way of reading the old/new distinction that launched the new labor history twenty-five years ago.

There is another virtue in the old labor history, at best dimly perceived by its early challengers, that has been brought sharply into focus by Peter Novick's book *That Noble Dream: The "Objectivity Question" and the American Historical Profession* (1988). I will have other reasons to draw on Novick's analysis, but here I want to emphasize the enlightening difference he finds between the way history and the social sciences emerged as modern academic disciplines around the turn of the century. Sociology, political science, and economics were reform-oriented and empirically grounded. They sprang from a rebellion against the nineteenth-century formalism of Social Darwinism and classical economics that enabled conservatives to divert attention from the real world of economic exploitation and urban-industrial crisis. In this assault, historical research was a key weapon—along with statistics, the empirical basis for exploding the deductive methodology of classical economics—and, for that reason, seized on so eagerly by John R. Commons and, at Johns Hopkins, by George E. Barnett.

The origins of labor history in institutional economics are well known. What Novick adds to the equation is an account of labor history's alternate parentage—the history profession proper. Professional historians identified a very different enemy, the amateur practitioners of narrative history; the "objectivity" they espoused to seize the ground from the amateurs was entirely conservative in effect. It was the brand of objectivity that could justify the dismissal of Edward Bemis from the University of Chicago on the grounds that his anti-business remarks betrayed "partisan unscientific methods"; he had "confound[ed] personal pleading for scientific thought." "History's principle contribution to society," says Novick, "was not policy advice, or advocacy, but legitimation." Amid the tumult of the Progressive Era, "professional historians were, with the most partial and insignificant exceptions, serene and untroubled in their celebration of traditional pieties: an island of orthodoxy in a sea of heterodoxy."[9]

It would take a social revolution—of which those of us who came of age in the 1950s were the beneficiaries—before the profession would be a fit place to write about American workers. This hard truth in turn compels us to cast a more sympathetic eye on the Wisconsin School, not only because it did what professional historians would not or could not do but also because it was impelled by, and its scholarship shaped by, a fruitful tension between present and past—an issue to which I will return.

Most of us at that session in 1978 had encountered the old labor history at second hand, so to speak, in the classic books of Commons and Perlman and, probably more determining, in the institutional histories of Taft, Walter Galenson, and other latter-day practitioners of the Wisconsin School. But at least one, Herbert G. Gutman, had a more direct and personal experience, for he had done his graduate work at Madison. After a hard beginning at Columbia, Madison in the early 1950s was in many ways a liberating place for Gutman. The progressive spirit was still very much alive, there was a lively bunch of left-wing fellow students to pal around with, and, of course, a famous history department. But someone with Gutman's interests actually had not much to choose between there, and he had to settle for the political historian Howard K. Beale. Gutman did have an alternative. Selig Perlman tried to recruit him, arguing among other things that history was an "Anglo-Saxon profession" and no place for a Jewish kid from New York. Gutman liked Perlman and took an economics minor with him, but he stuck with history as his subject, notwithstanding the difficult time he was having with Professor Beale. On finishing his coursework Gutman fled back to New York, where he spent the next five years working on his thesis very much on his own.

Why had he not gone over to Perlman? For reasons that I think were fundamentally *disciplinary*. Gutman must have felt that the proper way to write labor history was as the historian, not the labor economist, would write it. What this precisely entailed—the skills of the historian's craft, the liberating absence of a fixed disciplinary construct on labor's past, and examples by the best historians of that golden age of what might be aspired to—is difficult to sort out, but why the historian's discipline attracted Gutman and other graduate students (like myself) is captured as well as anywhere in a passing remark he made about the master's thesis he had done at Columbia. It was "conventional labor history, and I'm sure it bored my supervisor, Richard Hofstadter."[10] The new labor history, before it meant anything else, was work warranted by the historian's hand that took it up against boring the Hofstadters of this world.

That notion—to bring to labor history the particular genius of the historian's craft as it was practiced at that time—was most certainly in my mind as I began my dissertation on the steelworkers just when in his dissertation Gutman was grappling with the industrial conflicts of the 1870s. And on rereading *Steelworkers in America* (for a retrospective symposium on it), I am struck by how much of the new labor history it embodies—not only the open rejection of the Wisconsin School, so that the steelworkers themselves could be "the focus, not one or another of the institutions or events of which they were a part," but also some implicit sense of their "agency" as working people and close attention to community and ethnicity, the industrial context, and popular ideology. In one crucial respect, however, *Steelworkers* did not prefigure the new labor history. The book was about industrial struggle, but it was not radical history.[11]

During the 1960s a second revolution—the first was the demolition of "the Anglo-Saxon profession" against which Perlman had warned Gutman—overtook the historical discipline. During the 1960s some historians began to identify themselves as radical, and by the early 1970s they had scored a remarkable victory: Radical history had established its legitimacy within the profession. How that happened—the civil rights and antiwar movements that set things in motion, the various actors who took up the battle, the crisis within the profession, and the rise of the New Left—is by now reasonably well documented and understood. What turned the tide, argues Jonathan M. Wiener, was the collapse of any establishment monopoly over what constituted "good history," which,

Wiener insists, was how radical challenges had always been fended off. "The consensus about the boundaries of history that had consolidated historians' loyalties and commitments disintegrated," concludes Wiener. "During this crisis the profession redefined the field in a way that included radical historians' conceptions of the significant problems requiring study."[12]

Both Gutman and Montgomery came out of American left—Gutman by way of Jewish left-wing socialism, and Montgomery as a Communist trade-union organizer until he was blacklisted. Neither, notes Wiener, was conspicuous in the political battles that established radical history within the profession.[13] Their initial historical forays—the articles that came out of Gutman's dissertation and his summary essay "The Workers' Search for Power: Labor in the Gilded Age" (1963) and Montgomery's *Beyond Equality: Labor and the Radical Republicans, 1862–72* (1968) and, in the same year, his important article "The Working Classes of the Pre-Industrial American City"—make conceptual breakthroughs important for the new labor history.[14] But they do not explicitly stake out a radical position and most certainly are not programmatic statements on the order, say, of William Appleman Williams's *Tragedy of American Diplomacy* (1959), or Gabriel Kolko's *The Triumph of Conservatism* (1963), or Eugene Genovese's *The Political Economy of Slavery* (1965). But from that point onward, as activists of the 1960s abandoned the barricades for graduate schools, labor history became a central subject—one might almost say *the* central subject—of radical history. In Edward. P. Thompson's *The Making of the English Working Class* (1963), moreover, the new labor history found a model it sorely needed. Thompson's great book, once its message was assimilated, not only transformed labor history into working-class history but also, by emphasizing culture and consciousness, confirmed an orientation that Gutman and Montgomery had to some degree hit on independently.

How much his rejection of Perlman had been based on Gutman's politics we do not know, but what is clear is that, once the new labor history found its direction it discovered another use for the Wisconsin School as negative reference point. "The history associated with John Commons and Selig Perlman rested on a certain politics," remarked Gutman in a 1982 interview. "They sought to defend the liberal view of the trade unions as institutions essential for balancing inequalities in capitalist society without transforming that society." Gutman goes on:

> The new labor history also rests on a certain politics and is inspired by a distinctive philosophy of history. Much of it, in this country and in West-

ern Europe, developed in response to and out of the decomposition of classical Marxism. . . . This new labor history rejects the deterministic models that the labor history of the Old Left rested on. But it does not reject the vision of a more egalitarian and democratic society. Nor does it reject democratic socialism. I suspect that most of the new labor historians who have done significant work are men and women who define themselves, in one fashion or another, as socialists.[15]

We have to tread carefully here. Gutman is using his terms in the broadly encompassing sense that characterized radical history as it emerged in the 1960s—that is, with no doctrinal or party tests and open (as draft principles of the Mid-Atlantic Radical Historians Organization asserted in 1974) to "all persons who share its general perspective."[16] Within the boundaries set roughly by Stalinism on one side and New Deal liberalism on the other, anyone who identified him or herself as radical was, by definition, radical. With due regard for all kinds of exceptions and shadings, I want to argue that, in this ecumenical sense, radical history and the new labor history became one, or, to put it another way, radical historians have imparted to the new labor history its central tendencies as these exist today.

And, while much of what they brought to that task is of necessity hard to catch hold of, one seems of critical importance and quite specific: the way new labor historians situated themselves in relation to the past. To get our bearings here, we need to go back to Novick's book on the "objectivity question" and the historical profession. The founding generations staked their ground on the claims of objectivity—that it was the role of historians to approach the past in a detached way, that interpretation was to be judged only by how well it accounted for the facts, and that "historians, as historians, must purge themselves of external loyalties" and as best they could (an ideal to be striven for, they acknowledged, not an achievable goal) apprehend historical "truth." Their critics, Charles Beard and Carl Becker in the vanguard, answered that there was no such thing as historical truth. There was only what each generation could see through the lens of its own age, and the real vitality of history derived from what the historian brought to and needed from the past.[17]

It was still possible in the 1960s for conservative historians to attack New Left scholarship on the grounds that, as Irwin Unger wrote, it displayed "a contempt for pure history" and drew its questions not from "the *natural* dialogue of the discipline" but from "the outside cultural and political world."[18] In truth, however, that was a last gasp; objectivity had little hold on the profession even then. "The great majority of us believe that all historical writing is selective and thus suffused with value judgments,"

Carl Degler rightly says. "It is not the presence of intention or ideology in the historical researcher that is at issue—that can be taken for granted."[19]

But if intention or ideology can be taken for granted, they are present—or, to be more precise, salient in the historian's mind—in greater or lesser degree. Leon Fink captures neatly what I am trying to get at in an article entitled "The New Labor History and the Powers of Historical Pessimism." The article is devoted to the debate over whether the Knights of Labor really represented "a viable political culture"—a key matter for the new labor historians—but it is not so much Fink's argument itself as the way he casts it that interests me here. Why should conceding to the naysayers (in this case John P. Diggins and T. Jackson Lears) mean giving way to "the powers of historical pessimism"? It is only because of the historian's commitment to a particular historical vision. Fink's problem is that the Knights as alternative political culture in fact did not prevail, so at a minimum he must show that as real possibility, which he does with considerable ingenuity. Only by paying "close attention to context," he insists, will historians "understand why events took place as they did, *not as we would imagine them*" [my italics]. The historian, no less than the Knights of Labor, is the subject of Fink's ministrations, and this is because of a difference he finds between historians of an earlier generation and those of his own. In grappling with labor's historical defeats, the former asked "why *they* lost," the latter, "why *we* lost" [Fink's italics].[20] I want to argue that Fink has caught a key characteristic here, as, for example, when Jacqueline Dowd Hall and her fellow authors explain how their "own preoccupations" shaped the making of *Like a Family*; or when Patricia Cooper sits in judgment on the sexism and conservatism of the cigar makers she is studying; or, before he can launch his *Wages of Whiteness*, David Roediger feels he has to recount to the reader how he surmounted his racist upbringing in Cairo, Illinois.[21] If one imagined a subjectivity scale with they/we as the polar ends, all historians would find their place somewhere on that scale, but the new labor historians would surely cluster at the "we" end.

This was most certainly at the heart of why the new labor history had so remarkable a run over the past fifteen years. The three books I have just mentioned—*Like a Family, Once a Cigar Maker,* and *The Wages of Whiteness*—are entirely representative of those qualities of originality, empirical freshness, and sympathetic engagement that have made the best of American labor history the best in the profession. The record speaks for itself in the national prizes taken by labor histories in recent years and by the notable success of labor historians at landing jobs in a generally terrible job market.

The historical engagement that fired their scholarship was linked in turn to one further quality—a certain disengagement from the present. The new labor history, said Gutman, "refuses to look at a period of history simply as a precursor of the moment that we are currently living in." We have to remind ourselves of the historical "moment" at which the new labor history took shape in the 1950s and 1960s. The heroic age of industrial unionism was long past, the big unions seemed indestructible, industrywide collective-bargaining prevailed, and all that seemingly remained problematic were the gloomy implications of working-class affluence and mass culture. Under the circumstances, it was easy enough to disengage from an uninspiring present and see the past on its own terms—to rescue, in E. P. Thompson's memorable words, the obscure and bypassed victims of the Industrial Revolution "from the enormous condescension of posterity." The new labor history, insisted Gutman, rejected the Whig fallacy of history, whether the Wisconsin School's version or the Old Left's. "Freeing ourselves from the present in that way," said Gutman, "brings to life movements, brings to life a politics in the past, that was submerged by the crude presentism of the old labor history."[22]

To study the past in Thompson's terms was one of the hallmarks of the new labor history. But the status quo of the postwar era did more than turn younger scholars—to use Gutman's words—against "the crude presentism of the older labor history." For some of a more syndicalist bent, the perceived bureaucratic rigidities of contemporary labor-management relations served to goad their scholarship. Workers' control and rank-and-file militancy were themes defined in opposition to modern collective bargaining. It was Montgomery's view, in fact, that "the famous terms 'collective bargaining' and 'wage and job consciousness' have never been adequate to describe the aspirations of American workers" in the twentieth century. Thus he could applaud the New Deal for liberating workers from absolute managerial control but simultaneously condemn it for opening "a new avenue through which the rank and file could in time be tamed" and reducing "the labor movement to certified trade unionism." Montgomery had hopes when he wrote those words in 1977 that "workers' demands and struggles are once again breaching the confines into which managerial authority and the law seemed once to have restricted them."[23] As it turned out, the agents of change were not militant workers but militant managers. They have in the past decade driven union strength in the private sector down roughly to where it was at the start of the New Deal and reopened basic questions about the future of the labor movement.

What was also reopened were questions about institutions and power relationships that have always animated the Wisconsin School. Con-

sider, for example, Montgomery's *The Fall of the House of Labor* (1987).
Its roots are in *Workers' Control in America*, but whereas those essays
of the 1970s focused insistently on shop-floor struggle—"always emphasizing the initiatives of the workers themselves, rather than the ways in
which they were manipulated by those in authority over them"—the
book gives that struggle a rather different thrust. "Class consciousness
was more than the unmediated product of daily experience," Montgomery now says. "It was also a project," by which he means the sustained
efforts of "the 'militant minority' . . . to weld their workmates and neighbors into a self-aware and purposeful working class." The decisive role
they played, Montgomery argues, has been obscured not only by "the
common fixation on great leaders" but also by "'history from the bottom
up.'" And to understand the fate of workers' movements requires attention to "the changing structures of economic and political power fashioned by the evolution of nineteenth-century competitive industrial capitalism into twentieth-century imperialism."[24] The politics is nothing
like Selig Perlman's, to be sure, but the reorientation toward labor institutions and power relationships is unmistakable.

Having made that shift, however, Montgomery laid himself open to
the question of whether Perlman might have been right after all. Perhaps
"the famous terms 'collective bargaining' and 'wage and job consciousness'" did indeed describe the aspirations of American workers. So hard-
pressed did Montgomery find himself on that score in a symposium on
his book that he concluded that it was no longer possible to assume that
labor historians "shared . . . a common understanding of how history
should be written and what it is about. . . . On the contrary, we bring
sharply divergent, and often mutually exclusive, conceptions of society
to bear on the study of the workers' past." Montgomery's defense was
robust. "To say that class struggle has rarely, if ever, led to the overthrow
of capitalism by workers . . . is very different from denying the daily importance of class struggle." Without grasping "the ways that class has
shaped the actions of men and women in their making of history," social history is trivialized into a study of "the reproduction of everyday
patterns of sustenance and interaction," while the explanation of social
and political change is left "to those who write about the policy decisions
made by elites."[25]

To come to grips with these fundamental issues we have to be able
to debate them. And that can happen only insofar as others follow Montgomery's lead in placing institutions and power relations at the center
of labor history. There are many indications that this reorientation is
underway, but if I am right to argue that it must be seen as responsive to

changes in the contemporary environment, then there is also much about the new labor history as I have described it that makes that shift difficult. Consider, for example, how Leon Fink ends a recent article on the origins of the Wisconsin School: "Identifying vicariously with the eras of insurgency in American workers' past, while living amid a bureaucratic, defensive, and increasingly powerless labor union present, today's labor historians have not, in any institutionally creative sense, discovered a way to connect personally or politically to their subject matter."[26]

Or, in the same vein, this explanation by Eric Arnesen, a labor historian of the next generation, for why debates in the field have turned so acrimonious—a "war of words":

> One of the political ironies, and great frustrations, of being a radical academic in the 1980s has been the effective severing of the very connections between scholarship and politics that so many of us desire. Of what real consequence is the present generation of labor and social history? While presentist concerns have not guided our composite research agenda, many radical academics have carried out their work with the hope and expectation that their findings would be important, in some indirect way, to current-day politics, that a transformed understanding of the past—of actors, structures, and processes—could inform a politics of the present. But the rewriting of the past appears of little relevance in the political wasteland in which we live and work.[27]

One of the turning points in the battle over radical history twenty-five years ago, Jonathan Wiener tells us, was a reading Richard Hofstadter gave of the final chapter of his book manuscript *The Progressive Historians* at Harvard's Charles Warren Center in March 1968. The Warren Center, over which Oscar Handlin presided, was a bastion of conservatism. Hofstadter himself had been a high priest of the so-called consensus school dominating postwar scholarship. But now he sought some perspective on the political strife within the profession. "Once in each generation, the American people endured a crisis of real and troubling intensity"—the Civil War, the 1890s, the 1930s, and, now, the 1960s. In each case, observed Hofstadter, crisis gave rise to new ways of historical thinking. "The urgency of our national problems seems to demand, more than ever, that the historian have something to say that will help us," and it was the radical historians, he suggested, who had taken up that task and hence earned their place in the discipline.[28]

Can we say that, for the working people of America, there has been a crisis more serious since the Great Depression than the one facing them

today, with the labor movement in shambles, real earnings static or declining, and an economy undergoing restructuring of revolutionary scope?
Is this not a time that demands—to use Hofstadter's words—"that the
historian have something to say that will help us"? And here, for the last
time, I would like to invoke the old labor history.

In his account of its beginnings, Fink notes that in the tumultuous
1880s many labor economists identified themselves as Christian radicals
and ardent supporters of the Knights of Labor. As the Knights faded and
reaction set in, the engaged economists backed off and went their separate ways, with Commons, of course, ending up at Wisconsin. Fink treats
this, predictably, as a kind of sell-out, explained mainly by the academic
penalties the economists faced and their adoption of a new stance as
experts rather than advocates. All of this works well enough for Fink's
particular concern with the problem of the "intellectual" in the labor
theory of the Wisconsin School. But he bypasses the main story, that it
was in this later phase, in response to the crisis of the 1890s and the
emergence of modern trade unionism, that real historical research began
and a coherent analysis was fashioned. I think it is fair to say that, in
Hofstadter's terms and for its own time, the Wisconsin School fulfilled
the historian's role of having "something to say that will help us."

We need to bear that lesson in mind. I don't think we can afford to
bemoan the fact that we live in a "political wasteland" and let it go at
that. In confronting our own crisis, by bringing to bear what we know as
historians, we might be surprised by how fruitful an intellectual endeavor
we have entered. Who knows? We might even find the viable synthesis
that will finally replace Selig Perlman's.

Notes

1. Shelton Stromquist, "Perspectives on Labor History: The Wisconsin School
and Beyond," *International Labor and Working-Class History* [hereafter *ILWCH*],
no. 39 (Spring 1991): 83.

2. See, for example, Sean Wilentz, "Against Exceptionalism: Class Consciousness and the American Labor Movement," *ILWCH*, no. 26 (Fall 1984): 1–36; Michael Kazin, "Struggling with Class Struggle: Marx and the Search for a Synthesis
in U.S. Labor History," *Labor History* 28 (Fall 1987): 497–514; William Scranton,
"The Workplace, Technology, and Theory in American Labor History," *ILWCH*,
no. 35 (Spring 1989): 3–34; and Eric A. Arnesen, "Crusades against Crisis: A View
from the United States on the 'Rank-and-File' Critique," *International Review of
Social History* 35 (1990): 106–27. The introduction of gender has opened an entirely new dimension of debate, further complicated by the linkage of gender and
theories of language and discourse. See, for example, Joan W. Scott, "On Language,
Gender, and Working-Class History," *ILWCH*, no. 31 (Spring 1987): 1–36; Ava

Baron, ed., *Work Engendered: Toward a New History of American Labor* (Ithaca, 1991); and Mary Jo Buhle, "Gender and Labor History" and Alice Kessler-Harris, "A New Agenda for American Labor History: A Gendered Analysis and Questions of Class," both in *Perspectives on American Labor History: The Problems of Synthesis*, ed. J. Carroll Moody and Alice Kessler-Harris (DeKalb, 1989): 55–79, 222–32. The last-cited book grew out of a famous conference at Northern Illinois University in DeKalb in 1984 that signaled the breakup of any consensus among the new labor historians. For assessments of the DeKalb conference, see Kessler-Harris, "A New Agenda," 217–25; Michael Frisch, "Sixty Characters in Search of Authority," *ILWCH*, no. 27 (Spring 1985): 100–103; and Eric Foner, "Labor Historians Seek Useful Past," *In These Times*, Dec. 12–18, 1984, 11.

3. There had, in fact, already been an account using the old/new distinction: Thomas A. Krueger, "American Labor Historiography, Old and New: A Review Essay," *Journal of Social History* 4 (1971): 277–85.

4. "Herbert G. Gutman, "Work, Culture, and Society in Industrializing America," *American Historical Review* 78 (1973): 531–88; David Montgomery, "Workers' Control of Machine Production in the Nineteenth Century," *Labor History* 17 (Fall 1976): 485–509.

5. David Brody, "The Old Labor History and the New: In Search of an American Working Class," *Labor History* 20 (Winter 1979): 111–26.

6. Alexander Saxton, *Indispensable Enemy: Labor and the Anti-Chinese Movement in California* (Berkeley, 1971), ix.

7. David Brody, "Philip Taft: Labor Scholar," *Labor History* 19 (Winter 1978), 22. The issue includes a bibliography of Taft's writings (130–36).

8. Howard Kimeldorf, "Bringing the Unions Back In (or, Why We Need a New Old Labor History)," *Labor History* 32 (Winter 1991): 91–103, and "Responses," 104–27, in particular those by Michael Kazin, David Montgomery, and Bruce Nelson.

9. The quotations in this paragraph are from Peter Novick, *That Noble Dream: The "Objectivity Question" and the American History Profession* (New York, 1988), 62, 63, 68, 70.

10. Interview with Herbert Gutman in *Visions of History*, ed. Henry Abelove et al. (New York, 1983), 188. On Gutman's training, in addition to the interview cited, I rely on Ira Berlin, "Introduction: Herbert G. Gutman and the American Working Class," in Herbert G. Gutman, *Power and Culture: Essays on the American Working Class* (New York, 1987), 3–69.

11. David Brody, *Steelworkers in America: The Nonunion Era* (Cambridge, Mass., 1960).

12. Jonathan M. Wiener, "Radical Historians and the Crisis in American History, 1959–1980," *Journal of American History* 76 (Sept. 1989): 434. The key responses are by Christopher Lasch, John Higham, and Carl N. Degler (457–70).

13. Wiener, "Radical Historians," 410–11. On their radical backgrounds see the interviews with Montgomery and Gutman in *Visions of History*, ed. Abelove et al., 170ff, 188ff.

14. David Montgomery, "The Working Classes of the Pre-Industrial American City," *Labor History* 9 (Winter 1968): 3–22.

15. Gutman quoted in *Visions of History*, ed. Abelove et al., 200.

16. Draft principles of the Mid-Atlantic Radical Historians Organization are reprinted in the *Journal of American History* 76 (September 1989), 487–88; see also

the Introduction in *Towards a New Past: Dissenting Essays in American History*, ed. Barton J. Bernstein (New York, 1967), ix–x.

17. Novick, *That Noble Dream*, 1–3, offers a definition of objectivity; for the battle joined between conservatives and relativists, see especially chapter 8. The classic exchange is between Thomas Clarke Smith and Charles A. Beard in the *American Historical Review* 40 (April 1935): 439–44 and 41 (Oct. 1935): 74–87.

18. Irwin Unger, "The 'New Left' and American History," *American Historical Review* 73 (1967), quoted in Wiener, "Radical Historians," 426.

19. Carl Degler, "What Crisis, Jon?" *Journal of American History* 76 (Sept. 1989): 469.

20. Leon Fink, "The New Labor History and the Powers of Historical Pessimism: Consensus, Hegemony, and the Case of the Knights of Labor," *Journal of American History* 75 (June 1988): 115–36 (quotations on 134 and 136); responses by Diggins and Lears with Fink's rejoinder on 137–61.

21. Jacqueline Dowd Hall et al., *Like a Family: The Making of a Southern Cotton Mill World* (Chapel Hill, 1987), xvii; Patricia M. Cooper, *Once a Cigar Maker: Men, Women, and Work Culture in American Cigar Factories, 1900–1919* (Urbana, 1987), 3–7; David R. Roediger, *The Wages of Whiteness: Race and the Making of the American Working Class* (New York, 1991), 3–5. The autobiographical bent is not limited to labor historians, of course, but seems to be a general tendency among radical historians, as, for example, the interviews conducted by *Radical Labor History* and then gathered into *Visions of History* edited by Abelove et al.

22. Gutman in *Visions of History*, ed. Abelove et al., 200. In this and the following paragraphs I draw on passages in "Labor History, Industrial Relations, and the Crisis of American Labor," *Industrial and Labor Relations Review* 43 (Oct. 1989), 15–16.

23. David Montgomery, *Workers' Control in America* (New York, 1979), 5, 165.

24. Montgomery, *Workers' Control*, 4; Montgomery, *Fall of the House of Labor* (New York, 1987), 2.

25. David Montgomery, "Class, Capitalism, and Contentment," *Labor History* 30 (Winter 1989): 125–26, 131, 137. Montgomery was responding in particular to the criticisms of Sanford M. Jacoby (106–10), Michael Kazin (110–13), and Robert Zieger (121–25).

26. Leon Fink, "'Intellectuals' Versus 'Workers': Academic Requirements and the Creation of Labor History," *American Historical Review* 96 (April 1991): 420.

27. Eric Arnesen, "Crusades against Crisis," *International Review of Social History*, 35 (1990): 125; see also the relevant remarks of Kessler-Harris ("A New Agenda," 121–22) and Frisch ("Sixty Characters in Search of Authority," 121) about the bellwether DeKalb conference of labor historians in 1984. Kessler-Harris reported, "Though they hung, like stagnant air, over the conference, we never directly confronted the questions raised by a pessimistic view of the contemporary working class and organized labor's possibilities."

28. Wiener, "Radical Historians," 429–30. Hofstadter's is a nuanced discussion and one with greater reservations than Wiener's account allows. In fact, in the published chapter Hofstadter does not say "radical" historians, but in the context of the late 1960s he clearly had them in mind when he spoke of "committed historians." Richard Hofstadter, *The Progressive Historians* (New York, 1968), ch. 12.

2 The Future of the Labor Movement in Historical Perspective

Historians have been known, when they reach a dead end, to issue a ringing call to the profession to take up the task—and then move on. I myself have resorted to this dodge. But the challenge I issued in the preceding essay was not one I felt like evading. Or it might have been the fortuitous invitation soon afterward to deliver the Larry Rogin Lecture at the AFL-CIO's George Meany Center. Either way, the following essay, a revision of that 1993 lecture, represents a first, exploratory effort at applying labor history to current problems. It can also be read as a historical document because, unlike my practice in subsequent essays, in this one I do not elide contemporary references that might date the essay. The essay is indeed dated. It reveals one historian's view of the world as it seemed in the hopeful first months of the Clinton administration.

The title of this essay—"The Future of the Labor Movement in Historical Perspective"—is meant only half in jest. No one understands better than the historian that the future is beyond knowing, that there are no laws of history or cycles that can be plotted out and extrapolated into the future. But that does not mean history is irrelevant. Powerful continu-

Originally published in *Dissent* (Winter 1994): 57–66. Reprinted with permission.

ities connect past and present and to know what they are is to have guide-posts in times of trouble and confusion.

No reader has to be told that 1993 is a time of troubles for the labor movement. In 1975 union membership stood at an all-time high of twenty-two million. That translated into a union density in the nonagricultural sector of 28.9 percent, down only 3.9 points from the peak of 32.3 percent in 1953. Since then, unions have lost four million members, and union density has declined below 16 percent. If we count only private employ-ment, the labor movement is perilously close to where it was before the New Deal.

In the AFL-CIO president's view, this actually constitutes an achieve-ment. "We've maintained our membership in the most extraordinary combination of adverse circumstances," says Lane Kirkland, by which he doubtless means the hostile politics of the Reagan era, the militant antiunionism of American industry, and, most of all, the fiercely com-petitive markets and sweeping restructuring of enterprise that have un-dercut collective bargaining in America. Underlying these problems is the more fundamental crisis of a working class beset by declining real income and disappearing jobs. This is a new situation for a society that has known only sustained economic growth and hence probably beyond the histori-an's grasp. But the institutional issue—the question of the labor move-ment under severe stress—seems more tractable, with more from the past to guide us. This is not the first time of troubles for the labor movement, and its defeats and revivals are themes about which the historian ought to have something to say.

Among my fellow labor historians, it is unfashionable to invoke the name of Selig Perlman, whose *A Theory of the Labor Movement* (1928) most fully expounds the trade-union vision of Samuel Gompers. I would not want to defend Perlman's particular formulations, but in two ways Perlman's book still serves us well—first, by insisting on some organic link between labor movements and the working classes they serve and, second, by identifying the specific characteristics that this linkage has endowed on the American movement. Perlman uses the term *job-consciousness*, and I am content with it. By Perlman's definition, job-conscious unionism was maximalist in two ways: first, in advancing the job interests of workers, and, second, in placing the union at the center of that effort.

Did Perlman capture what unions in America do? Consider one of the thorniest bargaining problems facing unions today—the escalating costs of health-care coverage. This is not a collective-bargaining problem for other labor movements, not even Canada's. Why should it be in the

United States? The easy answer is of course that the U.S. lacks a national health insurance system. There was a time, in the waning years of the New Deal and during World War II, when universal health care was actively debated in this country. By then medical care, like old age and unemployment, had become elevated in the minds of Americans into a basic security right. Both wings of the labor movement—AFL and CIO— were robust advocates of national health insurance. Alan Derickson, a leading historian of workers' health and safety, has been struck by an apparent anomaly: that it was the "conservative" AFL, not the CIO, that stuck by national health insurance as its star waned in the postwar reaction signaled by the Republican congressional successes of 1946.[1]

The reason was that the AFL craft unions had a harder time figuring out how medical benefits might be incorporated into their collective-bargaining agreements. National corporations like General Motors and U.S. Steel had already instituted group insurance, and for the CIO unions it was mainly a question of forcing these benefits into the bargaining arena—not an easy matter by any means given the importance employers still attached to their welfarist programs but one effectively accomplished once the courts ruled that benefits were mandatory bargaining issues and the Steelworkers Union took a tough stand in the 1949 strike.

From this complicated story we can draw two conclusions. First, as to the outcome: medical benefits became almost universally a component of modern collective bargaining and as such emblematic of the maximalist tendencies of our job-conscious brand of trade unionism. Second, as to why we got that outcome: in this instance, most directly, it was the vacuum created by government inaction. That the labor movement fought so hard on behalf of national health insurance actually marked something of a break from a tradition going back to Samuel Gompers, who had always argued that it was the unions, not the state, that should protect the American worker. The underlying job-conscious logic, however, had not gone away. After all, national corporations already were providing for their employees through group insurance. The industrial unions could have left the matter there. That they did not do so stemmed at least partly from the ingrained logic that instructed American unions to maximize what they did for their members. It is no accident that collective bargaining in America—and not elsewhere—is burdened by the issue of medical insurance.

The larger implications—also no accident—can be seen in the statistical evidence gathered by Richard B. Freeman and James L. Medoff in *What Do Unions Do?* (1984). Unionized employers are not at any disadvantage in terms of labor productivity, say Freeman and Medoff. Just the contrary, in fact. But unions do take a bite out of profits. Union employers earn less on capital investment than do comparable nonunion employers—19 percent less in one survey cited by Freeman and Medoff. In a more recent study, Freeman and David Blanchflower find that this holds in international comparison as well. The costs of collective bargaining are substantially higher for employers in the United States than for those in any other advanced industrial country.[2] These findings sustain Perlman's notion of American job-consciousness, that is, extracting for workers the largest possible share of the returns of capitalist enterprise. We do not need to explore much further to understand the fierce resistance American employers have always thrown up against collective bargaining. From the standpoint of profit maximization, antiunionism is an entirely rational choice.

Money matters to workers, but so, at least equally, does treatment on the job. Indeed, it was here, over job rights, that Perlman drew his distinction between German and Anglo-American unionism. German unions concerned themselves "only with wages, hours, and watchful scrutiny of the operations of the governmental bodies administering labor laws and social insurance . . . [but] utterly failed to put in any bid for the dozens and dozens of job control rules achieved by American and English unions and designed to give the membership a right to the job, freedom from overwork and arbitrary discrimination, and the protection of their bargaining power."[3] The burden of Perlman's thesis was that this was not an accidental or minor feature of American trade unionism but historically rooted and central to its success. In continental Europe, by contrast, unions generally left shop-floor issues to state-mandated works councils, labor courts, or other public agencies. Elsewhere, as in Australia, work rules were informally regulated within the plant or, as in England (notwithstanding Perlman's Anglo-American category), through negotiation with autonomous shop-steward structures. The current controversy over the so-called adversarial system in American factories validates Perlman's insight. Workplace relations are a core union-management issue precisely because they are so intrusively a function of American unions.

Union people do not need a lecture on Selig Perlman in order to act in the manner he ascribes to them; the institutional context within which they operate tells them that. But the current crisis over American "competitiveness" has called job-conscious unionism into question. To emulate the Japanese and Germans, or to get the most out of advanced methods of production, the labor movement is told that it must embrace cooperative relations with employers. I have no quarrel with schemes that truly encourage employee involvement and flexibility, nor indeed with cooperative relations between labor and management wherever there are perceived common interests. If AT&T and the Communications Workers can work out a decision-sharing program, more power to them. But it is an illusion to believe that anything fundamental has changed in the basic relationship between labor and management in America. If there is a silver lining in the recent wave of plant closings and layoffs, it is to drive home the hard truth that no firm—not even corporate giants famed for providing job security, like IBM, or even those less pressed financially, like Proctor and Gamble and Eastman Kodak—can be counted on when the market turns bad and competition gets rough. Bank of America has a plan to convert its "platform" employees—the bank tellers, loan officers, and all the others who deal with the public in its branch banks—to part-timers so as to cut out benefits. Horror stories like this could be multiplied at will. Forced overtime is zooming while many jobs being created are for temporaries and contract workers—"disposable workers," the *New York Times* calls them. What the historical perspective I have described provides is a surer sense of labor's true course when passing circumstances (like those that prevailed during the 1980s) seem to say it should be doing something else.

From that historical perspective we can also find the means for remedying one of the great failings of the labor movement: articulating its mission to the outside world. The best term I can find to describe this is *industrial justice*, for what else is the claim that unions make on the profits of the firm but distributive justice for working people? And what else is protection on the job from arbitrary treatment but a kind of industrial justice? (This is not to mention the role of the labor movement as the single most important agent for social justice in our political system, as for example in the battle for national health insurance I have just described.) One would think that these truths would be shouted from the house tops, but we all know that, to the contrary, the labor movement is designated a special interest—Big Labor—and unions, or at any rate the people who lead them, are among the least admired in every public opinion poll. If the labor movement wants to find the language of industrial justice that it needs it would do well to study its own past.

Let me turn now to a range of more specific historical events that might serve as guideposts in labor's time of troubles. One concerns the structure of the labor movement. A couple of years ago I would not have thought this worthy of special comment. There has, fortunately, been nothing like the structural crisis in our own time that split organized labor apart during the 1930s. But two recent episodes in my own experience have changed my mind. One was an encounter I had with Staughton Lynd at a recent conference. Lynd is the grand old man of New Left labor historiography, still fighting the good fight for rank-and-file democracy as a labor lawyer in Youngstown. Lynd was advocating a shift of labor's orientation to community-based organizing—solidarity unionism, he called it. In the labor upsurge of the 1930s, he argued, this was the first impulse, and but for the imposition of national structures, with their bureaucratic tendencies, we might have had a militant and democratic brand of rank-and-file unionism more resistant to economic adversity and more capable of social transformation. While that possibility was cut short in the 1930s, Lynd contends that it "remains available as a model for how there could be built from below a labor movement of a different kind."[4] In my response I argued that what Lynd had captured in the early 1930s was real enough—community mobilization certainly did happen—but it had nothing like the significance he attached to it. In fact, those local movements never believed they could survive on that basis. They saw the logic of national structures. How else could they confront the great corporations like General Motors and United States Steel? Indeed, one of their main grievances, and a principal reason for the emergence of the CIO, was the AFL's resistance to their persistent demands for autonomous national unions.

That exchange with Staughton Lynd made me think again about the national-union structure that is the cornerstone of the American movement—not least because Lynd's view holds considerable appeal at the moment.[5] At one time, when it was a subfield of institutional economics, labor history was much concerned with the structure and government of unions. The definitive work in that vein—Lloyd Ulman's *Rise of the National Trade Union* (1955)—repays close reading for its brilliant analysis of how national unions emerged in response to the developing national labor and product markets of the nineteenth century. The national structure, in fact, was the institutional embodiment of job-conscious unionism and truly an example of form following function.

Today, a gauge of labor's weakness is the breakdown of national unity as employers whipsaw local unions and pit them against one another at plant-closing time. It may be that labor people do not need to be instructed on the importance of the movement's national-union structure, although had that been true we never would have seen Local P-9 out there on its own against Hormel in the Austin strike of 1985. In any case, a historical perspective on how and why the national-union structure developed most certainly is the best antidote against the siren song of Staughton Lynd's localism.

Beyond that, however, is a second, less obvious meaning in the history of labor's institutional development. Not long ago I contributed to a new entry on labor movements for the *Encyclopedia Britannica* covering North America, that is, the United States and Canada. Such an assignment generally gets reduced to country-by-country mini-essays, but I thought I could fashion an integrated account because my starting point was the singular fact that our national unions generally call themselves "internationals" and do so because they contain Canadian as well as U.S. branches. Everything in Canadian experience argued against a binational movement—Canada's antirevolutionary political culture, its fear of domination by the Yankee colossus, and rising Canadian nationalism. The contrary logic, however, simply overwhelmed the efforts to create a purely Canadian labor movement.

The enabling condition was the job-conscious grounding of the national-union structure, which rendered politics essentially beside the point and made economic empowerment the ultimate basis for action. If Canadian local unions chose to affiliate with the American nationals of their trade, they were welcome. And almost always they did—a kind of movement from below that set the process of integration into motion. The Canadian bodies were acting in just the way, and for the same reasons, that U.S. locals had when they earlier submitted to national organization.

From those nineteenth-century origins a true binational movement emerged, with the Canadians generally marching a half step to the rear. There was the same split over industrial unionism in the 1930s; a Canadian version of the National Labor Relations Act in 1944; anticommunist purges in 1949–50; and in the wake of the AFL-CIO merger in 1955, the Canadian Labor Congress the next year. At that point 70 percent of all organized workers in Canada belonged to AFL-CIO unions. Since then, the two movements have begun to disengage, but the 35 percent of Canadian membership still in AFL-CIO unions (as of 1990) suggests that integration is far from dead. And I would expect that if the movement toward a genuine common market should conclude with the ratification of the North American Free Trade Agreement, it will be accompanied by a strong revival of integrating tendencies.

The Free Trade Agreement, however, covers not only the U.S. and Canada but also Mexico. And that leads me, long way round I am afraid, to the historical guidepost I am trying to identify. Can the labor movement favor ratification—and the labor market it will create covering the whole of North America—if there is not the possibility for the kind of North American labor movement that we know job-conscious unionism to be capable of building? A Free Trade Agreement unaccompanied by at least the possibility of a true North American labor movement threatens basic premises about American trade unionism. Ought not those premises, just as much as jobs, be the basis on which the labor movement takes its stand on the Free Trade Agreement? On the trade-union conditions in Mexico today, the bleak facts are to be found in the report that Dan La Botz has done for the International Labor Rights Education and Research Fund: *Mask of Democracy: Labor Suppression in Mexico Today* (1992).

Collective-bargaining rights are nothing to brag about in this country either, and that brings me to a final area—labor law reform—where I think history has something useful to say. The Wagner Act marks a great divide for American labor, one we will probably never be able to re-cross. This is because the law is grounded in fundamental American principles of free choice and free association. When the Congress saw fit in 1935 to convey those rights to workers it helped set in motion the great organizing drives that led to the unionization of American basic industry. So we tend to forget that the Wagner Act is ultimately not about the rights of unions but about the rights of workers. This fact caused—and continues to cause—the labor movement considerable grief. It immediately compromised the freedom of the AFL to assign jurisdictions and of its affiliates to make contracts with employers; both were subordinated to the prior right of workers to choose representatives through the majority-rule provisions in the law. Beyond that, the distinction drawn between workers and unions—a distinction that would have been utterly inadmissible to Samuel Gompers—goes a long way toward explaining Taft-Hartley, massive regulation of the internal affairs of labor unions, and crippling restraints on their organizing activities, as, for example, in the recent *Lechmere* decision (1992), the denial to organizers of virtually any right to enter company property. That the law is about the rights of workers is what has given it moral force, however, and that needs to be recovered from the past.

So far as the Bill of Rights is concerned, pronounced the American Civil Liberties Union in its 1937 annual report, "The greatest gain of all has been the establishment of labor's rights under the National Labor Relations Act." The law was "in effect a civil liberties statute." The ACLU could say that because although the right to organize might not itself have been specifically grounded in the First Amendment, it was inextricably linked to the constitutional rights of free speech and assembly. This relationship was underlined by the Senate investigation launched by Robert

La Follette into violations of civil liberties soon after passage of the Wagner Act. La Follette fastened on the widespread reliance on industrial spies,
the stockpiling of munitions, the maintenance of private armies, and all
the dirty tricks companies used to intimidate workers and prevent them
from exercising their rights. Not only did these revelations immobilize
the open-shop camp but they also elevated labor's struggle to a battle for
civil liberties.

But, beyond that, the Wagner Act was at the heart of a great transformation in the meaning of constitutional rights taking place under the New
Deal. "Perhaps it is time to think of civil liberty as protection *by* the state
rather than protection *against* the state," wrote John Dewey in 1936.[6] The
record of the American Civil Liberties Union—it had initially opposed the
Wagner Act on traditional libertarian grounds—is a perfect indicator of
this remarkable but little-noticed shift that was the precondition for the
civil rights revolution of the 1960s. In the 1930s, however, it was labor's
rights that occupied center stage. Listen to Roger Baldwin of the ACLU
speaking in 1938: "However important or significant may be the struggle for the political rights of fifteen million Negroes; however important
or significant the defense of religious liberties; of academic freedom; of
freedom from censorship of the press, radio or motion pictures, these are
on the whole trifling in national effect compared with the fight for the
rights of labor to organize."[7]

We don't have to swing all that way back to capture the essence of
what Baldwin is saying. If we can move labor rights back on to the same
plane as civil rights, then for how much longer would Congress continue to wink at the fact that any employer prepared to use all the legal tricks
an expensive, union-busting law firm can deploy (and doesn't mind violating the law and absorbing the back-pay penalties) can defend his union-
free environment against all comers? Such cynicism is tolerable only
because we have lost sight of the law's original intent and of the essential truth still written into it—that it is about achieving "full freedom of
association" for workers.

The world being what it is, restoring that truth will not by itself do
the trick. Huge interests are invested in keeping the law as it is. One need
only contemplate the solid front being assembled to defend management's right to fight strikes by hiring permanent replacements to real-
ize how monumental a political undertaking it would be to accomplish
real labor law reform. American trade unionists have not—in our political system have never had—the weight to pull off a feat of this magnitude. But if they cannot ever expect to achieve the social voice that
Canadian unionists, say, have gained through the New Democratic Par-

ty, the U.S. movement has its own kind of political moment, not one that it creates but one that, when it occurs, can be seized on. The New Deal was such a moment; the Clinton administration may be another. Facile historical parallels are not my game here. What I am after is a particular historical guidepost embedded in the way the Wagner Act came about in the first place.

Let me begin with recent events. Last March [1993] the new Democratic administration established the Commission on the Future of Worker-Management Relations, the so-called Dunlop Commission after its chair, that old pro John T. Dunlop. Labor law reform thus has come on to the national agenda, not, however, by a route calculated to give much comfort to AFL-CIO strategists. What the Clinton administration has in mind are not the interests of organized labor, or even particularly the basic rights of workers under the law, but bigger fish— nothing less than American competitiveness in the global economy. The key arena, says Labor Secretary Robert B. Reich, is the workplace, and the goal, "high-performance work practice." This calls for job training, gain sharing (so workers are rewarded for working harder and better), and above all cooperative and flexible labor-management relations. Workplace reform is what energizes the Clinton administration. The link is explicit in the charge to the Dunlop Commission as well as in everything heard from the Clinton people ever since. High-performance work practice demands the rethinking of American labor law.

The labor movement cannot feel it has any inside track to the White House. Yes, Clinton made the expected sympathetic statements and symbolic gestures, most recently lifting the ban on rehiring the air controllers fired by Ronald Reagan in the 1981 strike, but labor and the administration are on opposite sides on the North American Free Trade Agreement, and the AFL-CIO cannot count on the White House when the chips are down on the striker replacement bill. About the union role in workplace reform, administration leaders have become exceedingly cagey. "Unions are O.K. where they are," says Commerce Secretary Ron Brown. "And where they are not, it is not yet clear what sort of organization should represent workers." And Labor Secretary Reich, who had earlier alarmed business with talk about leveling the playing field between labor and management, said: "The issue for me is worker voice. Workers need a voice at the workplace. I'm flexible about where that voice comes from or how it's expressed."[8] Chilling words for the labor movement. So, are its prospects bleak or not?

The resemblance to what transpired during the New Deal is, in fact, uncanny and in two particular ways. First, labor relations reform became attached to broader economic goals. In the Great Depression, of course, no one worried about American competitiveness. The mass-production system then seemed unassailably the best there was or indeed could be. But bad labor relations did produce a different kind of drag on the economy. Section 1 of our labor law still enshrines the New Deal economic thinking that made the Wagner Act saleable in 1935: "Inequality of bargaining power . . . tends to aggravate recurrent business depressions, by depressing wage rates and the purchasing power of wage earners in industry and by preventing the stabilization of competitive wage rates and working conditions within and between industries." Then the big issues were consumption and deflation; today, competitiveness.

The other similarity between then and now is scarcely less important, namely, that the Democratic administration not be seen as partisan to organized labor. Roosevelt came into office with no special ties to labor unions, no commitment to legislation for them, and no clear understanding of what it was they wanted or needed. Reich's statement on labor representation quoted above echoes Roosevelt's evasiveness, only FDR said it more pungently. As far as he was concerned, workers ought to be free to choose any representative they wanted, whether it be an individual, a union, the Royal Geographic Society, or the Akhoond of Swat. The Wagner Act—the heart of which was to settle that issue—was not administration legislation, and on the whole Roosevelt and his key people were more impediments than otherwise as the battle unfolded and the measure took shape. FDR signed on to Senator Wagner's bill only after passage was imminent. Exactly how the Clinton administration will position itself of course we don't know, but it will have its own reasons, just as FDR did, to want to stay at a distance from organized labor in the coming battle over labor law reform.

Lacking class politics as we do, Americans are strongly inclined to put the labor movement down as a special interest (and one that makes more than its share of enemies at that). Winning something of real magnitude like the Wagner Act in 1935, or changing it today, means somehow surmounting that fundamental constraint. That's what the New Deal accomplished, first, by attaching labor's interest to unimpeachable national economic goals and, second, by creating an environment at once sympathetic to labor's cause—without Roosevelt, make no mistake about it, there would have been no Wagner Act—yet not tainted by special-interest politics. It just may be that Bill Clinton's will be the second administration to bring off this rarest of conjunctions in American labor politics.

Going back to the origins of the Wagner Act offers one further guide-post worth bearing in mind now that the machinery for labor law reform has been set in motion. Once adopted, the Wagner Act took on a kind of constitutional mantle, subject to amendment (as by Taft-Hartley and Landrum-Griffin); over the years it acquired a massive superstructure of interpretation and case law, but its fundamentals were seemingly beyond history. Only occasionally does an apparent anomaly arise to remind us that the labor law came out of a particular time and was premised on a specific set of industrial conditions, as, for example, in the current vogue for employee involvement, the fact that labor-management shop commit-tees (if they deal with the terms and conditions of employment) are des-ignated under Section 8a(2) as company-dominated labor organizations.

The recent *Electromation* decision (1992) affirming Section 8a(2) in this respect has had a bracing effect, unsettling employers and tempting some of them to think that maybe the status quo is not so desirable af-ter all. What kind of law is it that prohibits a form of labor-management interaction that promises to enhance high-performance work practice?

The stir over Section 8a(2) suggests a broad interest—not least from the Clinton administration and the Dunlop Commission—in consider-ing alternative forms of workplace representation. Just because 8a(2) is woven into the entire fabric of the law, much more is going to be at stake than the revision or repeal of a single provision. It will behoove the la-bor movement to know its history when the debate is joined.

The Clinton administration is surely right to believe that fresh thinking is called for. Being the policy wonk (if I have the correct, inside-the-beltway word) that he is, Clinton appoints commissions, calls con-ferences, and consults experts. Roosevelt had a different style. He left the wonking to others, but he knew how to preside over the policy fray and when to bring things to a conclusion. The two years leading up to the Wagner Act were preeminently a time of searching debate, just what the Clinton administration hopes to call forth with its Dunlop Com-mission (omitting, of course, the bloody industrial battles that drove the debate in Roosevelt's time).

The labor movement won that debate, and if we are entering a com-parable period, then there is one last guidepost to be sought from the past: what the union movement brought to the struggle that enabled it to pre-vail on the representation issue. It was not, certainly, labor's political muscle, which was punier in 1935 than it is today. Nor was AFL leader-ship any abler or more savvy. We have to remember that the CIO came after the Wagner Act, not before, and that it was William Green, not John

L. Lewis, who was labor's voice in Washington. What the AFL did have was a true and inflexible sense of what it wanted. It would have been easier, certainly more politic, to have compromised, which was what FDR wanted and what at key moments the AFL could have done. The source of its intransigence was, of course, the job-consciousness with which I began this essay.

In its time, employee representation was a plausible option, and the historian can readily imagine a past in which works councils became a dominant mode of labor representation. Repealing Section 8a(2) is also plausible, and one can imagine—our secretary of labor can certainly imagine—luxuriant new forms of representation once management is no longer required to stay at arm's length from labor organizations. But if American labor law is still about the rights of workers, are we prepared to see these rights cut into so as to make room for representational forms that invite employer domination or, alternatively, to make the state guarantor of these forms of representation?

As for the labor movement, has it come to the point where it is willing to see its functions truncated in the name of high-performance work practice? The labor movement cannot be opposed to reforms that make for better systems of work. In fact, it had not done so in the case of the Wagner Act. The workplace representation that emerged from that law met the needs of the mass-production system, which was why the law won the assent of American employers once it was in place. But in achieving this organized labor did not sacrifice what was essential to it as a job-conscious movement. This is the balance it must strike again in the days ahead. And if this excursion into history helps at all in that process, it will have been an effort well worthwhile.

Notes

1. Alan Derickson, "Health Security for All? Social Unionism and Universal Health Care, 1935–1958," *Journal of American History* 80 (March 1994): 1333–56.
2. David G. Blanchflower and Richard B. Freeman, "Unionism in the United States and Other Advanced OECD Countries," *Industrial Relations* 31 (Winter 1992): 80–94. The most recent research casts doubt on the linkage between unionization and higher productivity but underscores the conclusion that unionized firms are less profitable than nonunion ones. Barry T. Hirsch, *Labor Unions and the Economic Performance of Firms* (Kalamazoo, 1991).
3. Selig Perlman, *A Theory of the Labor Movement* (New York, 1928), 311–12.
4. Lynd's paper was subsequently published as the introductory essay in a collection of like-minded case studies, Staughton Lynd, ed., *"We Are All Leaders": The Alternative Unionism of the Early 1930s* (Urbana, 1996).

5. See, for example, Charles Heckscher, *The New Unionism: Employee Involvement in the Modern Corporation* (New York, 1988); Michael J. Piore, "The Future of Unions," in *The State of the Unions*, ed. George Strauss et al. (Madison, 1992), 387–410; and Alice Kessler-Harris and Bertram Silverman, "Beyond Industrial Unionism," *Dissent* (Winter 1992): 61–66.

6. Jerold S. Auerbach, *Labor and Liberty: The La Follette Committee and the New Deal* (Indianapolis, 1966), 210.

7. Auerbach, *Labor and Liberty*, 26.

8. Ron Brown and Robert Reich quoted in *The New York Times*, July 5, July 27, Aug. 8, 1993.

3 Labor's Institutional Sources of Expansion and Contraction

Chronologically, the following essay might seem anomalous in the scheme of this volume. Every other entry was written after my call for an applied labor history in 1992. This one predates that call by twenty-five years. It earns its place here for two reasons. First, it shares this book's spirit of applied scholarship. Second, the essay withstands, I think, the test of time. True, if I were writing the essay today I would situate myself differently, but Professor Barnett would still be my starting point. In 1967 I was writing in the afterglow of labor's New Deal triumph. Today we are back where George Barnett was in 1932. I, however, have the benefit of his misplaced prediction and hence grounds for thinking that, in the right environment, the labor movement remains as capable of robust response as it was seventy-five years ago.

On December 29, 1932, George E. Barnett, dean of Johns Hopkins labor economists, delivered the presidential address before the American Economic Association. His speech had an ironic ring, for, at the close

This essay originally appeared as "The Expansion of the American Labor Movement: Institutional Sources of Stimulus and Restraint," in *Institutions in Modern America: Innovation in Structure and Process*, ed. Stephen E. Ambrose (Baltimore: Johns Hopkins University Press, 1967), 11–36. Copyright 1967 by The Johns Hopkins University Press. Reprinted with permission.

of a distinguished career, Professor Barnett was consigning the subject of his scholarship to academic oblivion. Trade unionism, he said, was exercising "lessening importance . . . in American economic organization." Membership had fallen below three million, to where it had been fifteen years before. Professor Barnett traced labor's decline back beyond the Great Depression raging at the time of his address. Basic weaknesses had emerged during the previous decade, when for the first time the union movement had failed to capitalize on prosperity. Professor Barnett drew a dark conclusion: "I see no reason to believe that American trade unionism will so revolutionize itself within a short period as to become in the next decade a more potent social influence than it has been in the past decade."[1]

Yet inside of six months organized labor was resurgent. It recovered the losses of a decade in two years, gained another three million workmen between 1935 and 1938, and reached fourteen million members in a final surge during the war years. "Measured in numbers, political influence, economic weight, or by any other yardstick," the president of the U.S. Chamber of Commerce acknowledged in 1944, "labor is a power in our land."[2] It was a far cry from the future predicted by Professor Barnett in 1932.

His miscalculation suggests a way of looking at the modern labor movement. Its capacity for growth housed contradictory tendencies— surging at some points, quiescent or worse at others. The expansive tendency, intermittent at best since the early years, virtually expired during the 1920s and early 1930s. Nor would a close study of trade unions have predicted any resurgence, for the trigger was not in the labor movement but in the larger environment. Professor Barnett's pessimism in 1932 was well founded (and almost universally shared). He could not foresee the impending turn of events. Even had he done so, the recent past would not have suggested trade unions' capacity to respond to the opportunity granted by the Great Depression and the New Deal.

In the formative years of the late nineteenth century the labor movement shaped itself on a modest appraisal of its place in American society. Trade unionists were reacting against the grand vision of labor reformers who imagined a cooperative commonwealth encompassing all "producers" and ending the evil wage system. Trade unionists saw a harsher reality—a nation permanently divided into warring classes by the Industrial Revolution. But if American labor was class-conscious, it was so in a peculiarly American way. Wage-earners thought of themselves not only as workers but also as Catholics, Republicans, German Americans, Odd Fellows. Trade unionism could not override this welter of competing loyalties. Nor could it pursue goals other than those of members. American workers were, in Selig Perlman's phrase, "job-conscious." They confined their interests, as workers, to the terms of their employment. Voluntary associations that they were, trade unions could lead only where the rank and file would follow.

No one saw more steadily nor better articulated the consequences of these modest circumstances than did Samuel Gompers. Not that he repudiated his youthful dreams. "I believe with the most advanced thinkers as to ultimate ends, including the abolition of the wage system," he was still saying in 1887. But Gompers set those dreams aside and, eventually, left them behind. They were beyond his reach. Trade unions, said Gompers, should attend to the immediate and the possible, attempting "to work along the lines of least resistance; to accomplish the best results in improving the condition of the working people . . . each day making it a better day than the one that had gone before. . . . And wherever that may lead . . . so far in my time and my age I decline . . . to be labeled by any particular ism." In short, the pursuit of "more, more, more, now."[3]

The movement likewise tailored its methods to its limitations. Economic action, not politics, seemed labor's best hope. The union movement would be hard-pressed to marshal to the polls a membership already tied to the established political parties. Moreover, political engagement invited a congenitally hostile state into labor's sphere. As voluntary associations, finally, trade unions found little organizational benefit in legislative gains. Compulsory unemployment insurance, Gompers' successor William Green once warned, would "pull at our vitals and destroy our trade union structure." Collective bargaining, on the other hand, gave unions a continuing function, a claim on the members, and, at least for craft workers, the chance to leverage their skills to best advantage. Gompers elevated these considerations into ruling principles. His doctrine of "voluntarism" located the labor movement firmly in the private sector. Unions should never seek "at the hands of the government what they could accomplish by their own initiative and activities." Underlying this were assumptions Gompers had absorbed at Karl Marx's knee. "Economic need and economic betterment could best be served by mobilizing and controlling economic power."[4]

Pure and simple unionism, as Gompers' formulation came to be known, described a tendency rooted in American labor development. The earliest local unions, Philip Taft has shown, devoted themselves to economic action and quickly learned to resist the temptations of politics and reform. Starting with the International Typographical Union in 1852, local bodies of the same craft began to form national unions. It was further proof of the commitment to economic unionism. To function effectively in the economic sphere, labor organization had to parallel nationalizing American markets. To that end, national unions gradually evolved controls over membership standards, over strikes, and over collective bargaining. The prime institutions for economic action, national unions became the dominant units of American trade unionism. When it was formed in 1886, the American Federation of Labor recognized their supremacy in its basic laws.[5]

The next two decades validated the trade-union approach. Labor's stubborn attachment to politics and reform finally withered with the collapse of the Knights of Labor during the 1880s. Trade unions, meanwhile, attained institutional stability. In the 1890s they survived a major depression for the first time. When prosperity returned, the movement burst forward. Membership more than quadrupled in five years, and collective bargaining made notable headway. An expanding future seemed to lie before a movement (as Gompers had said) "founded on eminently practical questions."

At that point American trade unionism became the victim of a historical irony. Just as the movement crystalized on the basis of nineteenth-century conditions, its environment changed. The advent of mass-production industry sharpened managerial opposition to collective bargaining and undermined union control of labor markets. Trade unionism discovered itself barred from the heart of the American economy—the great industries characterized by mass-production technology and large-scale business organization.

The limitations of a movement shaped by pure and simple doctrine now stood sharply revealed. Labor unions operated *in*, not *against*, the economic setting. They lacked the capacity, or even the will, to resist the technological changes undermining craft strength. Nor had they any answer to the vast resources wielded by giant corporations. Yet the AFL was unenthusiastic about the antitrust movement, regarding business concentration as a product of economic evolution and not to be resisted. Only in bituminous coal and garment making, demoralized by hyper-competition, did trade unions take the initiative and try to come to grips with their industrial environment.

Nor was politics a lever that organized labor might use. Legislation to redress the balance between labor and management was out of bounds. "In the demand for collective bargaining labor has never asked that it be gained by law." This was the AFL's response to a 1919 bill providing for collective bargaining in industries engaged in interstate commerce.[6] Some issues did, of course, demand political answers. There was no other so-

lution to a hostile judiciary that issued strike-breaking injunctions wholesale and approved yellow-dog contracts. And when it came to controlling
the labor supply there was no other way of restricting the flow of immi-
gration or regulating child and women's labor. But even for these limited purposes the union movement had difficulty mobilizing politically.
Authority and money were concentrated in the national unions, not in
labor's political arms—the city centrals, the state federations, and the AFL
itself. Not much changed, even after labor's aggressive shift in 1906 to
electioneering for its friends and against its enemies.

That left only accommodation. The AFL wooed big business, first
in the National Civic Federation and then, in the 1920s, in a campaign
(using the model of the Baltimore and Ohio plan) for greater industrial
efficiency coupled with flag-waving patriotism. Neither effort had much
success, as Gompers' faith in economic power might have foreseen. Not
conciliation but a more robust response to economic reality was what
offered hope for American trade unionism. In a hostile environment, that,
too, proved beyond its capacity.

To begin with, there was the rule of trade autonomy—that is, the sov-
ereignty of national unions. That was a condition for their entry into the
AFL, reflecting the primacy of national unions as the power centers of the
movement. They had the right, Gompers said from the outset, "to do as
they think is just and proper in matters of their own trades, without the
let or hindrance of any other body of men." The Federation, Gompers reminded the delegates at the last convention he presided over, was "an organization that had no power and no authority except of a voluntary character."[7] Unionization depended ultimately on the national unions, and
they, for their own good reasons, balked at the task.

The national unions had taken shape—a model was Gompers' Cigar
Makers Union in the late 1870s—as vehicles for collective bargaining. That
institutional development militated against robust organizing once a stable membership was built up and dues placed on a sound basis. Should
money be diverted from servicing the membership to organizing the unorganized? Would the results justify the expenditure? The internal structure, reflecting the local markets in which many AFL unions operated,
often left much authority and income in the hands of local unions and
district bodies. Would they support organizing activities of little direct
concern to them? The unions had evolved a career leadership and a one-
party political system. Might not an influx of new members, especially
those not drawn from a union's normal area of operation, endanger internal stability?

The list of questions lengthened. Organizing drives in mass-production industries demanded a joint effort. Would other national unions cooperate and carry a fair share of the work? Not if the disastrous steel drive of 1919 was an example. Trade unions, as voluntary associations, depended on rank-and-file loyalty. The unorganized were largely recent immigrants and blacks. Might they not alienate the native-born unionists? Could mass-production workers show the discipline essential for rational strike action and collective bargaining?

These hard questions did not all bear, or bear with equal weight, on every decision. But responsible leaders always balanced the narrow interests of their existing organizations against the claims of the unorganized. In an era when, in any case, odds were heavily against success, that calculation restrained the national unions as organizing agencies.

So Professor Barnett rightly despaired of American trade unionism in 1932. Locked into the crafts, the movement had very limited reach. During the 1920s only the building trades flourished. Between 1920 and 1926, thirty-three unions, primarily in manufacturing, shrank in membership by nearly 60 percent. Nor was there any sign of reform. One observer in 1926 found most labor leaders "a curious blending of defeatism with complacency." A harsher critic in 1929 dismissed the AFL as "a life raft—though now beginning to get waterlogged—for skilled labor." Three years of depression reduced the movement by another half-million members and rendered even the strongest unions ineffective in collective bargaining.[8] At the end of 1932, as Professor Barnett observed, the labor movement, seemingly, faced a dark future.

——————

The next months abruptly transformed the trade-union environment. As the economy touched rock bottom, industrial workers finally lost hope in welfare capitalism and turned militant. During the early New Deal, a spontaneous push for organization developed. It was a sight, said William Green, "that even the old, tried veterans of our movement never saw before."[9] In Washington and key industrial states, administrations came to power that both from conviction and expediency championed the cause of labor. The rank-and-file upheaval and political changes together with the economic impact of the depression weakened the defenses of capital. Even the mightiest of corporations became vulnerable to unionization during the 1930s.

The labor movement was the beneficiary, not the agent, of the sudden turn in its fortunes. But as beneficiary, its response was robust. To have attacked the basic industries earlier, John L. Lewis admitted in 1935, "would have been suicide for organized labor. . . . But now, the time is ripe; and now the time to do these things is here. Let us do them."[10]

That decision was as rooted in the logic of trade unionism as had been the feebleness of earlier years. John L. Lewis represented, one writer noted in 1925, "the older type of labor executive, autocratic, more aggressive than penetrating, unreceptive to the new principle[s], a protagonist of simple unionism." Conservative in politics, a dictatorial union president, Lewis seemed in the 1920s, as one observer wrote, "the grand walking delegate, the glorified organizer, the perfect boss in American labor."[11] Yet John L. Lewis was the man who took the lead in pressing for action after the start of the New Deal. "It's middling tough for one who fought John L. so long and bitterly to pay this tribute," confessed a labor journalist in 1933, "but give the devil his dues. John turned out to be the only archangel among the angels with fallen arches of the A.F. of L. crowd."[12]

Ambition and personal drive assuredly infused Lewis's apparent transformation. He was, as Francis Biddle later said, very nearly a great man, but his efforts were wholly explicable in trade-union terms. That statement holds also for Sidney Hillman, David Dubinsky, Charles Howard, and the lesser unionists who gathered around Lewis. Observing them at the end of 1933, David Saposs found "no ideological difference distinguishing them from the old guard. . . . They differ from the old guard on the best way to take advantage of the opportunity presented by government intervention."[13]

The industrial-union group was responding, first of all, to an ingrained sense of obligation to the unorganized. Gompers had always insisted that the AFL spoke for all wage-earners not just union members. Even when it grew remote from the concerns of many craft union leaders they never could deny the goal of organizing the unorganized. The depression revived labor's sense of mission. In 1932 the AFL came out for public unemployment insurance, a startling departure from voluntarism. The mild William Green astonished the country when he threatened "forceful methods" to shorten hours and increase wages. "We have simply come to what we are determined shall be the end the road of suffering." That sentiment infused the advocates of industrial unionism. "The labor movement is organized upon a principle that the strong shall help the weak," John L. Lewis told the AFL convention of 1935. "Isn't it right that we should contribute something of our own strength . . . toward those less fortunately situated? . . . Organize the unorganized and in so doing you make the American Federation of Labor the greatest instrumentality that has ever been forged in the history of modern civilization to befriend the cause of humanity and champion human rights."[14]

But realism always mattered more than compassion. On that trade unionists of every stripe agreed. "A union should be regarded as . . . progressive when it brings about a new condition in industry through the exercise of its power," Sidney Hillman argued in 1928. "Policy and strategy are only the means to the end, and the end is the realization of power for the movement."[15] And for individual unions. "Steel was the key to understanding Lewis' policy," remarked his lieutenant John Brophy. "The mine workers would never be safe until steel was unionized. . . . Lewis and the UMW, intent on steel, were driven to create the CIO, because there was no other way to get the job in steel done."[16] The Amalgamated Clothing Workers and the International Ladies' Garment Workers were similarly situated. Both waged incessant battles against nonunion competition and hence saw specific benefits in the organization of related industries. The narrow considerations of pure and simple unionism weighed heavily in the thinking of industrial unionists.

So did politics. The emphasis on economic power by no means weakened, but politics now loomed larger. For one thing, more was at stake. The New Deal was responsive, providing that the unions flexed their muscles. The NRA's automobile code had worked out badly, Lewis observed, because labor weakness (in this case, the lack of a national union) permitted "the Recovery Administration and the White House to make decisions without fear of any successful challenge from the American Federation of Labor."[17] Lewis, Hillman, and Dubinsky represented the segment of the AFL that most relied on New Deal activism and hence, by political calculation, most favored a bigger labor movement.

Not all trade unionists agreed. Key craft organizations, indeed, grew more deeply entrenched in the face of challenge. Between 1933 and 1935 their contribution, either by way of money or cooperation, fell short of past attempts to organize basic industries. Threatened by the industrial unionists, they embraced more stubbornly the principles of trade autonomy and exclusive jurisdiction. The rights of even ineffectual national unions had to be respected and so did the jurisdictional claims of the crafts in mass-production fields. "We are not going to desert the fundamental principles on which [the craft unions] have lived and are living to help you organize men who have never been organized," Dan Tobin of the Teamsters bluntly told John L. Lewis at a climactic meeting in May 1935. That obstinacy only fired the sense of crisis among industrial unionists. "We were all convinced," recalled John Brophy about a strategy meeting

held soon after, "that in the temper of the times, there was a great opportunity to push forward . . . that if the delay was continued too long,
it would mean the opportunity would run out on us, and we would lose
a chance that only comes once in a long while." To exploit it the Lewis
faction formed the Committee for Industrial Organization. If opponents
construed doing so as an act of dual unionism, Lewis felt, so be it. His
were "not the objectives of someone else, but the declared objectives of
the American Federation of Labor."[18]

Only one question concerned him. What would work? For mass-production workers, Lewis answered, only industrial unions. The issue of
structure had once held key importance for radicals bent on transforming the labor movement. In the 1930s the matter became more practical.
Industrial workers—"mass-minded" as William Green had described
them—resisted being parceled out into separate unions. Nor was anything
less than a unified organization likely to make headway against the giant corporations. So rubber, steel, and auto unions had to be formed on
an industrial basis. Pragmatic in his view of the structural issue, Lewis
in late 1934 had offered a solution: Let industrial jurisdictions be granted on a temporary basis. The craft unions could exercise their claims later,
when mass-production unions would be on a firmer footing.[19]

From that point on, considerations of power—as characteristic of the
trade-union mentality as Lewis's pragmatism—dominated the dispute over
structure. Craft unions, after seeming to agree, quickly backed away from
Lewis's proposition. Could they exercise their jurisdictions after unionization on an industrial basis? Not if the new unions were strong enough to
prevent it. Craft unions knew that in the end it would be power, not legality, that would be determining. So the craft unions withheld their people
from the jurisdictions of the Auto and Rubber Workers at meetings of the
AFL Executive Council in early 1935. They had enough votes later in the
year to ratify that decision at the climactic convention in Atlantic City.
But a ballot could not settle this issue. The Lewis group had a vital interest and the means to pursue it. In the past, the AFL had always given in to
that combination—hence, among other things, the Mine Workers' own
industrial jurisdiction. Now, in the 1930s, the AFL faced a confrontation
of two power blocs with vital interests and no room for compromise. Giv-
en Lewis's stake in organizing the mass-production workers, ignoring the
AFL resolution against industrial unionism was a sound trade-union decision. Nor, curiously, was it inconsistent for craft chieftains such as William Hutcheson—himself a master of *machtpolitik*—to raise their hands
in horror over Lewis's violation of majority rule and exclusive jurisdiction.
In a decentralized labor movement, legality and power politics existed side

by side. The only surprising feature was that craft unions, without much regard for the constitutional niceties, read the industrial-union group out of the America Federation of Labor and so transformed the Committee for Industrial Organization into a rival federation.

Free as it was to experiment, the CIO drew heavily on the practices of American trade unionism. The organizing drives, of course, posed special, and to some degree new, problems. The mass-production workers were aroused, they were riven by racial and ethnic divisions, and the Wagner Act enabled them to choose among rival unions. In this situation, fresh tactics emerged. Yet with the exception of the "organizing committee" (such as the Steel Workers Organizing Committee), the CIO followed structural arrangements already in existence, and its effectiveness sprang mostly from characteristic features of the American movement. Strong treasuries enabled the CIO to throw funds into organizing, professionalization of union work meant a cadre of organizers was immediately available, and centralized leadership made for tactical decisiveness. "We're in a position to throw our weight about," John L. Lewis told subordinates after the United Mine Workers had reestablished itself in the coal industry. "We have some resources. We have some money and some manpower to put into a struggle of this kind."[20]

In one final way did the CIO capitalize on a characteristic strength of the established movement—its ability to exploit the American left wing. As voluntary associations in a pluralistic society, trade unions necessarily judged people by performance rather than by their politics and outside affiliations. Participants had only to adhere to one priority: Union objectives came first. Socialists had functioned in the labor movement on this basis for many years. And some who had suffered at the hands of John L. Lewis, radicals like John Brophy, Adolph Germer, and Powers Hapgood, swallowed their bitterness and went back to the Mine Workers. Germer, former secretary of the Socialist Party, quit, because, as he explained, it was a time for action, not talk. Another socialist, following a similar path into union affairs, agreed "that working in an economic organization we are likely to accomplish more now than working in the party, as it is now constituted."[21]

On the far left, it was true, there was a robust tradition of dual unionism, best exemplified by the Industrial Workers of the World. By the 1930s, however, this indigenous radical strain had been supplanted, except for fragments, by the Communist Party, whose relations with organized labor were determined not by historic tendencies of the American left but by instructions from Moscow. As it happened, the Party reverted to a policy of boring from within just as the CIO was emerging. John

L. Lewis was willing to accept even communists, not only because (as he said) he felt confident that he could control them but also because the labor movement could control them—their participation depended on devotion to trade-union objectives.

Because they operated as disciplined factions, communists were politically formidable wherever they became well entrenched. In the ensuing internal struggles, however, the issue was over control and not basic policies. When the communists won out it was because they persuaded the rank and file of their commitment to trade-union objectives—hence the successful union careers of men like Harry Bridges, Julius Emspak, and Ben Gold. Where they failed to do that, as in the United Automobile Workers and the National Maritime Union in World War II, the communists lost their hold.

With the onset of the cold war the question of priorities became acute. Following their divisive performance in the 1948 elections, communist-dominated unions were expelled from the CIO. They and their fellow left-wingers had already, however, made a mighty contribution to organizing the unorganized. By 1946 the CIO had prevailed in the mass-production sector of the economy.

That achievement, far-reaching as it was, did not exhaust labor's capacity to expand in a favorable environment. The AFL, far from crumpling, increased just as rapidly as did the CIO for the first decade after the split and then in the later 1940s began to outdistance its smaller rival. By the time of the merger in 1955 the AFL represented more than ten million workers, the CIO five million.

In mass-production industry the challenge had been for established national unions to invest in an organizational growth that would not accrue to them. Only the leaders of the CIO had managed to jump that gap—to think, as Sidney Hillman said, "in terms of the whole labor movement."[22] The others continued to put their own national unions first, as the logic of American trade unionism had always dictated. But that did not render them ineffectual; on the contrary, many AFL unions experienced remarkable growth after 1935. Between 1936 and 1941 the Machinists went from 105,000 to 284,000, and the building trades from 650,000 to 893,000. The Teamsters, never larger than 100,000 before 1933, reached 170,000 in 1936, 530,000 in 1941, and 1,300,000 in 1955. Of the six biggest unions in the early 1960s, four had been old-line AFL unions—the Teamsters, Machinists, Electrical Workers, Carpenters.[23]

Initially, these craft unions had concentrated on their contested ju-

risdictions in mass-production industries, but then the AFL unions began to look beyond their own crafts. Not every union, to be sure. "No
organizing campaign was put into effect by our International office to
recruit membership in wholesale lots," the Bricklayers' leadership reported in 1938. "We insisted that our unions function for the benefit of those
who had remained loyal to the organization through times of stress."[24]
But others, making their own trade-union calculations, began to look
farther afield toward lower-paid workers working by the side of skilled
men, toward related areas hitherto neglected, and, finally, even toward
accessible workers wholly unconnected with the main jurisdictions.

In part the expansionist logic was opportunistic. Workers who would
pay dues could be had for the taking. Thus a vice president of the butchers' union said, "I couldn't see much future in just working on Meat
Cutters and Packing House Workers, so I started on a campaign on the
Creamery, Poultry, and Egg Houses."[25] For some union leaders, especially of the younger generation, more membership provided its own justification. Economic change, as always, reshaped jurisdictional interests. The
Teamsters, for example, had represented only local delivery drivers when
intercity trucking became a major industry in the 1930s. Although President Dan Tobin was happy with local drivers—the so-called crafts—
Jimmy Hoffa and other Young Turks pushed the Teamsters into over-the-
road trucking, which employed more than a million workers in 1941. In
this instance the existing membership benefited strategically; in other
cases defensive reasons were in play. The butchers' union, hitherto limited in the retail field to meat cutters, began to organize food clerks, both
to protect its skilled men in self-service supermarkets and to fend off the
CIO retail union.

In 1934 the International Association of Machinists received jurisdiction over aircraft workers. At first the union acknowledged other craft
jurisdictions in plants. By 1938 the IAM was battling the CIO for the
aircraft workers and organizing "on the only basis that could be successful and that is, taking in all mechanics. . . . If this method of organization
is interfered with, the Machinists could not continue to organize in this
industry." So, ironically, CIO competition transformed this rival of John
L. Lewis into an industrial union in some areas. By 1952 more than a third
of the Machinists' membership was classified as production workers. The
next year the union dropped the constitutional distinction between journeymen and others. It had cut loose entirely from its craft origins.[26]

To forestall the CIO, AFL unions moved also into neglected fields.
The United Brotherhood of Carpenters, for example, had successfully
claimed the entire wood-products industry before World War I but with-

out any intention of actually organizing the wood workers. During the early New Deal, when new unions began to sprout in the Northwest, the Carpenters accepted wood workers as "B" members (with lower dues, fewer benefits, and restricted political rights). As soon as the CIO invaded, that foot-dragging ended. An amazing union fight ensued that included naval warfare between AFL and CIO boats patrolling the waters around Pacific sawmills.[27] As the CIO expanded beyond its original base, other AFL unions struck back. The Teamsters began to take in warehousemen; the Electricians, utility workers; and the construction trades, residential building workers.

The AFL rarely succeeded at the core of mass-production industry. But a vast peripheral field remained that was susceptible to—indeed, better suited to—the tactics of AFL unions, which were decentralized, with local unions dispersed across the economy and often equipped and motivated to carry on organizing work. Moreover, AFL unions serviced their locals less than centralized CIO unions did, so proportionately more income at the national level was available for organizing work.

Equally important was the strategic power that the Teamsters, for example, enjoyed once they gained a foothold in over-the-road trucking. Using "leap-frog organizing," the Teamsters in the late 1930s jumped from Chicago to St. Louis and Joplin, Missouri, and from Minneapolis to Kansas City and Omaha, swiftly organizing the intercity trucking industry. The same leverage was then applied to local truckers and, finally, to a wide range of businesses dependent on truck deliveries. "Once you have the road men," boasted Jimmy Hoffa, "you can have local cartage, and once you have local cartage, you can have anyone you want."[28]

Other AFL unions as best they could duplicated these pressure tactics. In the fight for the Northwest lumber industry, the Carpenters refused to handle products from CIO plants. "Why don't [CIO leaders] admit that a union is strong or weak depending on its power to boycott efficiently?" crowed the United Brotherhood. Boycott tactics enabled the Carpenters to recapture a substantial part of the Pacific industry despite a bad reputation and a resourceful CIO opponent.[29] The Amalgamated Meat Cutters exerted the same kind of pressure on meat-processing plants, and to some extent so did other craft unions moving into manufacturing fields. Although techniques varied, including both collusion and muscle, organizing employers was a key to AFL success, notwithstanding that the Wagner Act, in principle, gave workers a free choice on union representation.

So the favorable environment evoked two patterns of growth from the labor movement: industrial unions for the basic industries and diversified organizations outside the mass-production sector. The CIO and AFL approaches had never been entirely distinct, and they increasingly over-lapped after the initial industrial-union surge. Together, they lifted the labor movement to eighteen million members by 1955 (three million outside the AFL and CIO).

In the end this analysis returns to where it began. Professor Barnett had foreseen a dim future for the labor movement in 1932. Twenty years later his gloomy words began to find an echo among union experts. In 1953 the labor editor of *Fortune,* Daniel Bell, announced that "U.S. labor has lost the greatest single dynamic any movement can have—a confidence that it is going to get bigger. Organized labor has probably passed its peak strength."[30] Although disputed at the time, Bell's prediction proved to be prescient. Union density peaked at 28 percent in 1953 and then began to decline notwithstanding that, in absolute numbers, the labor movement was still growing by an average hundred thousand members a year.

Obviously, the movement has not come full circle. Organized labor is incomparably stronger today [1967] than it was thirty-five years ago. Powerful national unions now have a voice in the decisions that govern the economy. The AFL-CIO exerts an influence in politics beyond Samuel Gompers' dreams. In its internal affairs organized labor has become more flexible and realistic. It would be hard to imagine the AFL-CIO being held back, as was the AFL before 1935, by rigid rules of exclusive jurisdiction and trade autonomy. And the organizing techniques devised by AFL unions continue to have a significant measure of success in nonmanufacturing areas.

Yet as a whole the labor movement finds itself at a standstill. Growth has stopped because organized labor has again run into an unfavorable environment. And, as earlier, the movement is stymied. Its greater strength notwithstanding, it still lacks the capacity to change an adverse environment. It cannot forestall the new technology that is cutting into its base in many fields. It cannot reverse legislative and court decisions, beginning with the Taft-Hartley Act, that have taken away some key advantages. It can do little to change the circumstances that make the major unorganized areas—the South, agriculture, and white-collar work—resistant to trade unionism. As before the depression, organized labor has found no answer to adversity.

The foregoing line of analysis does suggest two predictions beyond what Professor Barnett saw in 1932. Should the environment become more favorable—possibly as a result of racial progress in the South, new labor patterns in agriculture, automation in white-collar fields, or, more dramatically, from political or economic upheaval—the labor movement would show itself able to seize the opportunity. It is equally probable that, should another breakthrough occur, trade unionism would not depart from the basic direction charted by Samuel Gompers any more than the movement did in the 1930s. By drawing these two lessons from recent labor history, of course, a third is ignored: not to make predictions and so avoid being found in error, as is the case with Professor Barnett, by future historians.

Notes

1. George E. Barnett, "American Trade Unionism and Social Insurance," *American Economic Review* 23 (March 1933), 1, 6.

2. Eric Johnston, *America Unlimited* (New York, 1944), 176.

3. Philip S. Foner, *History of the Labor Movement in the United States*, 4 vols. (New York, 1947–65), 2:177; U.S. Commission on Industrial Relations, *Final Report and Testimony*, 11 vols. (Washington, D.C., 1916), 2:1528; Louis D. Reed, *The Labor Philosophy of Samuel Gompers* (New York, 1930), 18ff.

4. James O. Morris, *Conflict within the AFL* (Ithaca, 1958), 138–39; Reed, *Labor Philosophy of Gompers*, 118; Samuel Gompers, *Seventy Years of Life and Labor*, 2 vols. (New York, 1925), passim.

5. Philip Taft, "On the Origins of Business Unionism," *Industrial and Labor Relations Review* 17 (Oct. 1963): 20–38; Lloyd Ulman, *The Rise of the National Union* (Cambridge, Mass., 1955).

6. Morris, *Conflict within the AFL*, 38.

7. Reed, *Labor Philosophy of Gompers*, 149; Bernard Mandel, *Samuel Gompers* (Yellow Springs, Ohio, 1963), 524.

8. David Saposs, *Left-Wing Unionism* (New York, 1926), 115–16; Irving Bernstein, *The Lean Years* (Boston, 1960), 84, 385; Sumner Slichter, "The Current Labor Policies of American Industries," *Quarterly Journal of Economics* 43 (May 1929): 427.

9. American Federation of Labor, *Proceedings* (1933), 8.

10. Saul Alinsky, *John L. Lewis* (New York, 1949), 80.

11. Cecil Carnes, *John L. Lewis* (New York, 1936), 139, 145.

12. Oscar Ameringer, clipping, n.d. [1933], John Brophy Papers, Catholic University of America.

13. David Saposs, "The New Labor Progressives," *New Republic*, Jan. 24, 1934, 300–302.

14. Chester M. Wright, "Labor Unfurls Battle Flags," *Nation's Business* 31 (Feb. 1933): 13–15; A.F.L., *Proceedings* (1935), 541–42.

15. Sidney Hillman, "Labor Attitudes," in *American Labor Dynamics*, ed. J. B. S. Hardman (New York, 1928), 292–93.

16. John Brophy, *A Miner's Life*, ed. John O. P. Hall (Madison, 1964), 249; David Saposs, "Industrial Unionism," *Journal of Political Economy* 43 (Feb. 1935): 81; AFL, *Proceedings* (1935), 539.

17. Philip Taft, *The AFL from the Death of Gompers to the Merger* (New York 1959), 104.

18. AFL Executive Council Minutes, April 10–May 7, 1935, 124; John Brophy Memoir, 553, Oral History Collection, Columbia University.

19. On this point see David Brody, "The Emergence of Mass-Production Unionism," in *Change and Continuity in Twentieth-Century America*, ed. John Braeman et al. (Columbus, 1964).

20. John Brophy Memoir, 555.

21. Marx Lewis to Adolph Germer, March 31, 1934, Germer Papers, University of Wisconsin.

22. Matthew Josephson, *Sidney Hillman* (New York, 1952), 382.

23. *Monthly Labor Review* (May 1964): 506.

24. Walter Galenson, *The CIO Challenge to the AFL* (Cambridge, Mass., 1960), 521.

25. David Brody, *The Butcher Workmen: A Study of Unionization* (Cambridge, Mass., 1964), 248.

26. Galenson, *CIO Challenge*, 507; Mark Perlman, *The Machinists: A New Study of American Trade Unionism* (Cambridge, Mass., 1961), 93, 212.

27. Robert Christie, *Empire in Wood* (Ithaca, 1956), chs. 8, 19, 20; Galenson, *CIO Challenge*, ch. 11.

28. Ralph James and Estelle James, *Hoffa and the Teamsters* (Princeton, 1965), 100 passim.

29. Christie, *Empire in Wood*, 302.

30. Daniel Bell, "The Next American Labor Movement," *Fortune* 47 (April 1953): 204.

4 Section 8a(2) and the Origins of the Wagner Act

In 1967, when the preceding essay was written, little was heard about shop-floor rights, not as yet even among New Left champions of participatory democracy. Quite forgotten were the New Deal battles over workplace representation that had paved the way for the modern labor movement. Twenty-five years later, as the Clinton administration was getting started, those battles were stirring again, provoked now by exponents of a "high-performance" workplace. Readers of chapter 2 will recall that this issue figured in my first attempt at applied labor history. My passing remark that history had something to say about the provisions of the labor law governing shop committees caught the attention of the conveners of a conference on labor law reform called in preparation for Clinton's Commission on the Future of Worker-Management Relations. The following essay is my contribution to that conference.

Nearly sixty years have passed since the passage of the National Labor Relations Act in 1935. So far removed are we from that time, remarked the legal scholar Paul Weiler at the law's fiftieth anniversary, that the sides are reversed. Management is content with it while organized labor

This essay originally appeared in *Restoring the Promise of American Labor Law*, edited by Sheldon Friedman et al. Copyright © 1994 by Cornell University. Used by permission of the publisher, Cornell University Press.

thinks that maybe the best thing would be to scrap the law and return to "the law of the jungle."[1] Is any purpose to be served by revisiting those distant days when the Wagner Act was hailed as labor's Magna Carta? Consider the apparent anomaly of the recent *Electromation* decision—that shop committees, which many in industry and government consider to be essential for fostering employee participation, are actually illegal under Section 8a(2) of the law.[2]

Even today, Section 8a(2) remains pristine, without the usual encrustation of amendment and case law of a sixty-year-old provision. The National Labor Relations Board acknowledged as much in the *Electromation* case, which it decided primarily by an examination of legislative intent. Senator Wagner is quoted extensively, and close attention is given to the successive wording of Section 8a(2), which in the end prohibits not only employer domination in, but also interference with, the formation or administration of labor organizations as well as any support, financial or otherwise.[3] The reach of Section 8a(2) is determined by how the law defines "labor organization," and here, too, there is no mistaking the legislative intent. In its final wording, Section 2(5) leaves no shelter from the prohibitions of Section 8a(2) for workplace forms of representation that are concerned with the terms and conditions of employment.

To the amici in the case who argued that changed industrial conditions call for a more flexible approach, the board responds rather plaintively that it cannot do so "when congressional intent to the contrary is absolutely clear."[4] One can understand why, in a law committed to fostering contractual relations between employers and employees, Congress would be anxious to prevent the suborning of a collective bargaining agent by its opposite number. But what can Senator Wagner and his colleagues have had in mind by the radical constraints written into 8a(2) and 2(5), constraints so sweeping that they apply to employer actions not tainted by antiunion animus (*NLRB v. Newport News Shipbuilding Co.* [1939]) and to employee organizations not aspiring to collective bargaining (*NLRB v. Cabot Carbon Co.* [1959])? That Section 8a(2) was not inadvertent became altogether certain when Congress undertook the Taft-Hartley overhaul of 1947. The House adopted a provision permitting employers in the absence of a certified bargaining agent to form or maintain employee committees for the purpose of discussing matters of mutual interest, including the terms and conditions of work. The provision was rejected in conference, specifically (so Senator Taft reported) because the conferees wanted the prohibitions in Section 8a(2) left "unchanged," and so they have remained ever since.[5]

What has changed is an industrial environment that now places a premium on employee involvement. This takes various forms, from quality circles to production teams and up to, at its most advanced, shop committees like the ones disestablished by *Electromation*. At stake, argued some amici in that case, was American competitiveness in the global economy. And when the Clinton administration came into office a few weeks later, lo and behold, that was exactly the position it took. Workplace reform is what the Clinton administration has in mind when it calls for labor law reform and is explicit in the charge it gave to the Commission on the Future of Worker-Management Relations, the so-called Dunlop Commission after its chair, John T. Dunlop.[6] The goal is a system of workplace representation more varied and collaborative than is permissible under existing law.[7]

The drift of the administration's thinking is underwritten by the most authoritative of academic voices. In *Governing the Workplace: The Future of Labor and Employment Law*, Harvard scholar Paul Weiler commits himself to a specific reform: Employee Participation Committees mandated by law for every workplace with twenty-five or more workers. Taking as his model the German works-council system, he proposes that these committees be elected from within the plants, authorized "to address and respond to the broad spectrum of resource policies of the firm." And yet, powerfully argued and wide-ranging as it is, Professor Weiler's book contains but a single sentence suggesting that this is a choice that the country considered once before and rejected when it chose the Wagner Act.[8]

In what follows, I propose to retrace that history, taking as my central argument that what was at issue—and what accounted for the sweeping language of Sections 8a(2) and 2(5)—was a systemic choice being made between rival forms of workplace representation. My method will be, in the fashion of the historian, to follow a basically chronological course, stopping along the way at major junctures—five by my count—that bear on our current debate over labor law.

Section 7(a)

The first juncture in this history came in June 1933 with the passage of the National Industrial Recovery Act, the early New Deal's misbegotten effort to fight the Great Depression through the cartelization of American industry. Included in the Recovery Act was Section 7(a), which said that employees had the right to organize and bargain collectively through representatives of their own choosing and in exercising that right to be free from the interference, restraint, or coercion by employers or their agents.

Only historians might get excited about the question of how Section 7(a) got into the Recovery bill and why, once in, it stuck. For our purposes the main thing is to understand that although Section 7(a) might have been more or less a historical accident, something like 7(a) was certain to have been enacted because the principles it embodied had already prevailed in an ideological struggle going back at least several decades.

In a world of great industrial enterprises and armies of workers, individual rights steadily lost ground to the more urgent claims of collective action, climaxing in the Norris-LaGuardia Anti-Injunction Act of 1932. There was no audible dissent to the statement of public policy that workers should have the right to organize and bargain collectively. Some of the language of Section 7(a) is lifted bodily from Norris-LaGuardia, and the rest is paraphrased. There in Norris-LaGuardia, moreover, are the key doctrinal words of the Wagner Act—"full freedom of association" and "actual liberty of contract." That latter phrase disposes of an expiring legal theory—*actual* liberty of contract is what public policy demands, not the fiction of freely contracting individuals—and the declaration that the yellow-dog contract is unenforceable in the federal courts drives the conclusion neatly home.

Section 7(a) advanced beyond Norris-LaGuardia only insofar as inclusion in the NRA codes of fair competition made it more than a mere statement of public policy. In fact, inclusion in the codes was not much of an advance, and ineffectuality is the standard theme of 7(a) history—of the hopes of industrial workers raised and then crushed by the resistance of powerful corporate interests and the fecklessness of the New Deal. All too true. Yet, from the perspective of our own failed labor law, Section 7(a) can be seen in a quite different light, for what it also demonstrated was the power of ideas whose time had come. Today, the underlying principles are obfuscated by all the encumbering amendments, court and NLRB doctrine, and institutional interests engulfing the labor law. Section 7(a) stood quite alone, little more than an assertion of principles but for that very reason capable of summoning forces that brought the Wagner Act into being. That leads me to a second historical juncture: the response of open-shop employers to Section 7(a).

Employee Representation

The damning term commonly used by historians, and by critics at the time, was "company union," but we will do better to accept the term advanced by employers and one more functionally descriptive—"employee representation plan" (ERP), or, in some companies, "works council." This was a *workplace* system of representation, normally limited to single plants and not contemplating contractual relations. That the works council would be the first line of employer defense was obvious from the jockeying over Section 7(a) before the Recovery Act was enacted, and while industry lobbyists had not gotten what they wanted—a proviso protecting "existing satisfactory relations"—they went away satisfied that 7(a) was loose enough to encompass employee representation.[9] The passage of the law triggered a tremendous rush to put ERPs into effect, sometimes with a charade of employee consultation, mostly not. The cynical motives were all too plain.

Yet employee representation also had quite respectable, well-founded roots in the advanced management thinking of the time. The most direct line into New Deal history runs back to John D. Rockefeller Jr., the very earnest heir to the Standard Oil fortune. One of the Rockefeller properties, the Colorado Fuel and Iron Company, had fought a bitter strike for recognition by the United Mine Workers that ended in the Ludlow Massacre of 1914. Rockefeller claimed ignorance of the firm's affairs, only to be publicly exposed by evidence developed by the U.S. Commission on Industrial Relations, which at that time was investigating the nation's endemic industrial conflict. Embarrassed and chastened, he called in the Canadian industrial-relations expert (and later prime minister) W. L. Mackenzie King and between them they devised a representation plan for the Colorado mines. Thenceforth, Rockefeller became a fervent and vocal advocate, taking what he considered to be an advanced position in favor of industrial democracy during and after World War I. Subsequently, he financed the most important research and consulting operation of its kind in the 1920s—Industrial Relations Counselors, Inc.[10]

In early 1934, at the height of the battles over Section 7(a), the head of that group, Arthur H. Young, became vice president of labor relations at the United States Steel Corporation. From that perch Young did the strategic thinking for the national ERP movement. And in the Steel Corporation, with its two hundred thousand employees and preeminent place in American industry, he had a big stage for testing his program. We can get a taste of what Young thought he was up to from a statement of principle he was fond of quoting:

> The human element in industry is the factor of greatest importance. Capital cannot exist without labor and labor without capital is helpless. The development of each is dependent on the cooperation of the other. Confidence and good will are the foundations of every successful enterprise, and these can be created only by securing a point of contact between employer and employee. They must seek to understand each oth-

er's problems, understand each other's opinions, and maintain that unity of purpose and effort upon which the very existence of the community which they constitute and the whole future of democratic civilization
depend.[11]

So how did employee representation fare in practice? The plans commonly called for joint councils, with management and labor accorded an
equal number of votes and a majority required for any action—a trans-
parent management veto, of course. The details varied, but the small print
invariably left the final word to management. At International Harvester, where Arthur Young ran things in the early 1920s, representatives who
stepped out of line got a hard lesson; they were laid off or transferred.[12]
When labor costs had to be cut, as in the sharp recession of 1920 and 1921,
ERPs found themselves bypassed and thereby deflated; in general, on
wages and the basic terms of employment they got nowhere. Yet it was
also true that, after the shakeout of plans initiated only to satisfy a wartime directive or to counter a unionizing threat afterward, employee representation developed a good deal of staying power. The necessary ingre-
dients seem to have been, first, a personnel department capable of curbing
line supervisors; second, an established and progressive benefits program;
and, third, company willingness to expend the energy needed to keep the
plans from winding down into inactivity.[13]

With Section 7(a), of course, there was a new influx of firms not truly
committed to the ERP concept, and this was, as Arthur Young later acknowledged, a problem at United States Steel, which had long been skeptical of Rockefeller's plan.[14] Yet the incentives to make ERPs work were
now vastly higher than before; moreover, over the next two years they were
much rewritten and generally made more autonomous of management.

For those in the labor movement wondering whether shop committees might not be a halfway house toward unionization, the answer from
the history I have been describing is a qualified yes. The evidence suggests that ERPs did foster local leadership and, insofar as they failed to
produce results, did educate workers and strengthen the case for collective bargaining by outside unions. An extreme instance is to be found in
the Akron rubber industry, where, after fostering its Industrial Assembly for fifteen years, Goodyear unilaterally dropped its share-the-work
program and reimposed an eight-hour day in 1935, opening the floodgates
of unionization. At Arthur Young's showcase in U.S. Steel, ERPs in the
sheet and tin plate subsidiary moved in 1935 (over his objections) toward
federation. The next year, ERPs at the basic steel subsidiary were seized
by union adherents, who, at a critical moment, went over to the CIO.[15]

For those wondering whether the ERP experience of sixty years ago suggests that shop committees can inculcate the company loyalty and commitment we now prize, the answer is also a qualified yes. A pretty fair test would be how ERPs fared after 1935 when they came up against CIO challenge and NLRB disestablishment orders. At companies that had made a long-term investment in progressive labor relations—DuPont, for example, or AT&T—independent unions did take root. When Leo Troy surveyed this little-noticed sector in 1961 he estimated a membership of 1.5 million in two thousand organizations (although he could not specify what percentage of these actually stemmed from the pre-Wagner Act ERPs).[16] And, in light of current union-avoidance strategies, Sanford Jacoby has more recently given respectful attention to firms whose welfarist policies worked and who retained the loyalty of their workers.[17]

As to the big question of whether employee representation had ever offered a viable policy choice, the answer is, again, a highly qualified yes. The reality was that because employers had moved so swiftly, the works councils already occupied the ground. At their peak in 1934 they covered probably three million workers, more than did the unions and, in the mass-production sector where they were most heavily concentrated, very much more. That ERPs existed, that they were functioning, and that enormous business interests stood behind them had to be taken into account. But there was another fact that also had to be taken into account. With 7(a), employee representation was no longer a private affair. On the contrary, it was deeply entangled in a massive program of industrial regulation, which brings me to my third historical juncture.

Workplace Representation and the State

In deciding how to square employee representation with Section 7(a) the country was also deciding what kind of authority the state should assert over labor-management relations. The context in which this happened nearly defies recapturing, for the National Industrial Recovery Act represents America's one serious romance with a corporatist economy. Each of some four hundred codes of fair competition contained, in addition to comprehensive trade regulations, not only Section 7(a) but more or less detailed provisions on wages, hours, child labor, and a variety of working conditions. A profusion of agencies sprang up to interpret and enforce all this. Overseeing the whole was the National Recovery Administration; then, under its aegis, the National Labor Board of 1933–34; the successor National Labor Relations Board of 1934–35; regional labor boards and a few industry labor boards; other labor boards under code authority; and, finally, a whole host of NRA compliance and code committees. The question of collective-bargaining rights was enmeshed in this bureaucratic jungle, and intermingled with other, sometimes more pressing, NRA concerns with enforcing code labor standards and settling industrial disputes. In this state of confusion—or, if you will, open possibilities—what was at issue was not only the definition of bargaining rights but also the scope of state responsibility.

The Wagner Act embodied one resolution—of course, the one that prevailed. But consider another. The powerful men at the head of the National Recovery Administration, General Hugh Johnson and his general counsel, Donald Richberg, took the view that Section 7(a) called for a "perfect neutrality" between forms of labor organization. The company union was just as legitimate as the trade union. It was the employer's duty to deal with both insofar as each was freely chosen by employees, but not to grant exclusive recognition to either. The Johnson-Richberg plan contemplated multiple representation, protection of the rights of minorities and individuals, no bar against company unions, and a kind of local option over the actual forms of collective bargaining—let the parties decide what they wanted, so to speak.[18]

Where this might have led is best seen in the president's automobile settlement of March 25, 1934. The initiating crisis was entirely emblematic of the time. The AFL unions were demanding representation elections leading to exclusive recognition. The companies answered that their workers already had representation through ERPs but that they were willing to deal with (but not recognize or contract with) unions for their own members. Fearful that a national auto strike might set back economic recovery, President Roosevelt intervened and crafted a settlement embodying the Johnson-Richberg principles but adding the principle of proportional representation. Employers agreed to bargain with "the freely chosen representatives of groups," joined in a bargaining committee on a "pro rata" basis.

To enforce the settlement the president appointed a special Automobile Labor Board with final and binding authority. The board first dealt with the backlog of discrimination cases and then in early 1935 administered elections for what it called "bargaining agencies" for every auto plant in the country (except Ford), the members of which were identified by affiliation and selected by a complex process to reflect the plantwide vote. Each member acted as grievance person for his or her own district and for broader issues sat on the bargaining agency.[19] The agencies replaced ERPs, generally adopting their district lines, and became, in effect, the state-mandated works councils Paul Weiler has in mind.

We might therefore pause to ask what light that experience throws on the current enthusiasm for alternative forms of workplace representation. Insofar as the works councils in Professor Weiler's plan are intended to supplement existing collective bargaining protections and not to be in lieu of them as was the case in 1934, to that degree, of course, the two situations are not comparable. In fact, the auto works councils displayed very much the same weaknesses as the ERPs they replaced, with members of the bargaining agencies complaining that they had no independent base of power and no claims on management beyond the right to be heard.[20] Yet in the responsibilities they imposed on the state, the auto works councils do have a certain relevance for labor law reform.

The Automobile Labor Board, employing a staff of more than a hundred, administered plant elections across the industry, and, on unresolved grievances, it began to function as a kind of labor court. Who would be charged with these responsibilities if the law mandates, or even only authorizes, works councils? If freedom of association remains basic doctrine in the law, as I assume it will, does it fall to the NLRB to police works councils and shop committees against the threat of company domination and manipulation? If so, by what criteria? At the time, auto unionists castigated works councils for being powerless, but the historical record also reveals them calling the councils "government unions." Most certainly, labor law reformers will want to think carefully about what functions the state will be undertaking if it becomes the author of alternative forms of workplace representation.

The auto settlement was a real alternative at the time. President Roosevelt put it forth as the basis on which "a more comprehensive, a more adequate and a more equitable system of industrial relations may be built than ever before. It is my hope," he added, "that this system may develop into a kind of works council in industry in which all groups of employees, whatever may be their choice of organization or form of representation, may participate in joint conferences with their employers."[21] Think about what our labor relations might have looked like had FDR's "hope" come to pass.

The Path to Section 8a(2)

We come now to my fourth historical juncture—the moment of truth, so to speak—when Congress chose the path leading to the National Labor Relations Act. From the day Senator Wagner started the drafting process in early 1934, the basic strategy proceeded on two tracks, one leading to a viable framework for free collective bargaining and the other to the expurgation of the rival workplace representation system. For the latter purpose, a serviceable weapon was at hand in a principle already well established in railway labor law—that employer domination of labor organizations was a prohibited activity.[22] That was the very first problem to which Senator Wagner's team turned when it produced the sketchy initial draft dated January 31, 1934.[23]

How far to extend the curbs on employer domination, however, was not initially clear. The finished draft of the Labor Disputes bill (S. 2926) that Wagner submitted to the Senate on March 1 defined as labor organizations those existing for the purpose "of dealing with employers concerning grievances, labor disputes, wages or hours of employment." A more comprehensive phrase covering "other terms of employment" ought to be added, a key academic adviser, William E. Leiserson, wrote to Wagner. Otherwise, "The contention may be made that company unions may be kept in existence to deal with those terms of employment that are not covered in this sub-section defining 'labor organization.'" Similar reasoning prompted Leiserson's colleague Edwin H. Witte to urge the addition of "employee representation committee" to the definition of labor organization.[24] Logic went in one direction but politics in another. In early May, Senator Wagner lost the initiative in the Senate Education and Labor Committee, and the powerful chair, David I. Walsh, pushed for a more accommodating bill.

Walsh's substitute permitted employers to initiate and influence, but not interfere with or dominate, employee representation committees (and other forms of labor organization); to pay employee representatives for their time (but not contribute financially to labor organizations); and it entirely dropped the handling of grievances as a defining function of protected labor organizations. Had the preservation of employee representation been their primary concern, employers should have welcomed the Walsh substitute. But, of course, their real interest was not protecting ERPs but fending off genuine collective bargaining. In a key concession, the Walsh substitute dropped the explicit duty to recognize and bargain with representatives of employees. But employers could not be sure that they would not be faced with exclusive bargaining agents selected by majority rule, all of which was permissible at the discretion of the industrial adjustment board created by Walsh's bill.[25]

After it was too late, Arthur Young remarked that he thought employee representation and collective bargaining were compatible and could function side by side.[26] If that was Young's belief he had blown his chance. Employers, Young included, fought the Walsh bill and helped kill it in June 1934. In a revealing letter, Young figured that time was on his side. Efforts to enforce 7(a) could be stonewalled until it expired, and there would never "be given as good a chance for the passage of the Wagner Act as now [June 16, 1934]."[27]

But time proved to be on Wagner's side, not Young's. The steam went out of the NRA experiment; the 1934 congressional elections swept out the Republicans and created the most liberal Congress in memory; and the futile struggle to enforce Section 7(a) exposed ever more sharply the cynicism behind the fine talk about the rights of workers (not least by the publication of Young's damaging letter). There is no way of understanding what drove the campaign for a labor law without taking account of management's opposition—above all, to the prospect of genuine collective bargaining with independent unions—and, of course, the miscalculations that come so easily to people bent on preserving their power.

When Senator Wagner resumed the battle in the 1935 Congress, the gloves were off. The definition of employer domination of a labor organization became airtight, as did the meaning of labor organization in Section 2(5). On reading the draft, Secretary of Labor Frances Perkins noted that labor organizations were defined as organizations created for the purpose of *"dealing with* employers." Would not *bargain collectively* be the preferred term? No, came the vehement rejoinder from Senator Wagner's key aide Leon Keyserling. If Perkins's amendment were accepted, "then most of the activity of employers in connection with the company unions we are seeking to outlaw would fall outside the scope of the Act. If, as employers insist, such 'plans,' etc., are lawful representatives of employees, then employers' activity relative to them should be clearly included, whether they merely 'adjust' or exist as a 'method of contact,' or engage in genuine collective bargaining. It is for this reason that the bill uses the broad term 'dealing with'."[28]

The architects of the bill were entirely clear about the fact that they were forcing a systemic choice, hence the insistence on retaining grievance handling as a defining function of labor organizations. Because employee representation plans are mostly "nothing but agencies for presenting and discussing grievances and other minor matters . . . to exclude the term 'grievances' particularly would exclude from the provisions of this act the vast field of employer interference with self-organization by way of such plans or committees."[29] This statement, in its remarkable negativity, defines the drafting strategy: Workplace organization is encompassed by 2(5) so it can be excluded in 8a(2).

So did the Congress not contemplate a need for workplace representation or recognize grievances as a legitimate expression of employee discontent? Of course it did, only not through company-dominated labor organization or—just as important—not by legislative enactment. The shaping of Section 8a(2) has to be placed in its true historical context, which was the massive NRA experiment that was in place during this entire period. (The Supreme Court killed it only on May 27, 1935.) By introducing separate labor legislation, Wagner was intent on an act of *disengagement* from that corporatist morass. The evolution of the law was driven by this intention. Thus the NLRB ended up a public board, not tripartite; free-standing, not associated with the Labor Department; concerned strictly with collective bargaining rights, not with mediating and arbitrating labor disputes; and endowed with independent, adequate powers of enforcement, which under the NRA had been utterly lacking.

To define the NLRB as quasi-judicial was not only empowering but also, in the free-wheeling NRA context, delimiting. It was this quite precise combination—of state authority powerfully mobilized yet narrowly applied—that gave the Wagner Act its distinctive cast and, indeed, its particular programmatic thrust. The law protected the right to organize and bargain collectively; collective bargaining itself remained free. Section 8a(2) is part of that great settlement, disengaging workplace relations from meddling NRA bureaucrats and leaving it in the realm of free collective bargaining.

Workplace Contractualism

This brings me to my final historical juncture. When collective bargaining began in 1936 and 1937 there was little argument about the contents of the first contracts: provision for shop stewards, a formal grievance procedure, and the principles of seniority in layoff and rehire, pay equity across jobs, and just cause in discharge and disciplinary actions.[30] The hallmarks of the unionized workplace were present at its birth. Where had they sprung from? From a history of shop-floor struggle accompanying, and in my view driving, the legislative history I have been describing. The starting point went back much before the New Deal to the emergence of mass-production technology and the parallel development of internal labor markets and hierarchical command structures. In the 1920s and even earlier, one can already spot the key elements in various firms—pay equity as job classification systems appeared, rules for dispensing job opportunity among permanent employees, due process in disciplinary matters, and a felt need for some formal mechanism for eliciting the views of workers and processing their grievances (which was, of course, the best argument for employee representation plans). The problem was that corporate employers were only imperfectly committed to what they themselves had created. And when the Great Depression struck, these failures became magnified in the minds of workers. Facing unemployment and speed-up, they had an enormous stake in predictable, rule-bound treatment.

The workplace events of the pre–Wagner Act era all moved in a common direction. Even at their most pliant, the employee representation plans marked a kind of beginning for the grievance procedure. The AFL unions strenuously resisted the ERP system, but given their impotence on the bargaining front they had little choice but to channel their energies into workplace organization. At General Motors, shop committeemen had won the right to process the grievances of union members well before there was any contract.

The sense of formal process inherent in these emerging workplace structures was fostered as well by the NRA's halting efforts at adjudicating violations of Section 7(a). Among the entitlements springing from these proceedings, most telling perhaps was seniority. One of the charges to the Automobile Labor Board had been to handle discrimination cases by testing discharges and rehires against fixed criteria that included marital status, efficiency, and seniority. Invoked for this specific purpose, seniority almost at once became a general entitlement, accepted as such by the Auto Board and the industry. When it signed with the United Auto Workers a month after settling the great Flint sit-down strike, General Motors took the position that it was embodying contract practices already in place. What remained implicit but was perfectly evident in future actions was that General Motors was satisfied that it was accepting a workplace system that met the requirements of a great manufacturer of mass-produced automobiles.

Now that we have arrived at the moment when that no longer seems to be the case, it might be well to bear in mind that, historically considered, the workplace contractualism now so much in disfavor represents a triumph of accommodation to the industrial world as it then was. So, perhaps more to the point, does the labor law. It left workplace representation to collective bargaining because it was confident of the result and swept out alternative forms of workplace representation because no compelling case was made for conserving them. A case has been advanced that Senator Wagner and his advisers, by empowering workers, thought they were laying the basis for high-trust cooperative workplace relations.[31]

Management harbored no such vision; running the plant was their job. The management rights clause in union contracts, as Barry and Irving Bluestone have been at pains to point out, stands as a monument to their determination.[32] In its heyday before the Wagner Act, the works council was never conceived to be of any serious relevance to better plant operations. Now that it is, we ought not to read the past as a cautionary tale but rather for what it tells us about how we earlier fashioned the right responses to our economic environment and, in particular, about what our labor law had contributed—and might once again contribute—to high-performance workplace relations.

Let me conclude by mentioning the fate of Arthur H. Young. In February 1937 the Supreme Court had not yet validated the Wagner Act, and Young was still trying to keep the ERPs at U.S. Steel going. Young was vice president in charge of labor relations, but he did not know that the chair of the firm, Myron C. Taylor, had been secretly negotiating with John L. Lewis since early January. On March 1, 1937, the astounding news broke that the steel corporation was recognizing the CIO union. After a decent interval Young resigned. He had thought himself ahead of the curve as a progressive labor manager, but in fact he had fallen far behind. He was not even in on the decision that launched collective bargaining in the steel industry.

Notes

1. Paul C. Weiler, "Milestone or Millstone: The Wagner Act at Fifty," in *Arbitration 1985: Law and Practice,* ed. Walter J. Gershenfeld (Washington, D.C., 1985), 37.

2. *Electromation, Inc. v. Teamsters Local 1049* (309 NLRB 1992).

3. In the original Wagner Act, the section is designated as 8(2), but for consistency's sake, and to avoid confusion, 8a(2) will be used throughout this essay.

4. The decision is reprinted in the *Daily Labor Report,* Dec. 18, 1992, E1–23. The quotation is in footnote 9. In its brief survey of relevant decisions, the board takes note (E6, 7) of the one serious departure from the strict construction of 8a(2) by the Sixth Circuit Court (*Scott & Fetzer Co.* [1982], *Airstream, Inc.* [1989]) and finds it wholly unconvincing. For a fuller survey of the judicial history of 8a(2) written under the shadow of the Sixth Circuit initiative, see Thomas C. Kohler, "Models of Worker Participation: The Uncertain Significance of Section 8(a)(2)," *Boston College Law Review* 27 (1986): 534–45. For a useful listing of the scholarly commentary on 8a(2), see the bibliographical note in Raymond L. Hogler and Guillermo J. Grenier, *Employee Participation and Labor Law in the American Workplace* (Westport, 1992), 174–75.

5. *Daily Labor Report,* June 8, 1959, D3 (in the text of *NLRB v. Cabot Carbon Co.* [1959]).

6. The commission's mission statement is reprinted in the *Daily Labor Report,* March 25, 1993, F1.

7. See the statements by Ron Brown and Robert Reich in the *New York Times,* July 5, July 27, Aug. 8, 1993, and by commission members Thomas Kochan and Paula Voos in the *Daily Labor Report,* April 30, 1993, A17, May 4, 1993, C2.

8. Paul Weiler, *Governing the Workplace: The Future of Labor and Employment Law* (Cambridge, Mass., 1990), 213, quotation on 285.

9. See, for example, "Memorandum to Members of the Employment Relations Committee, National Association of Manufacturers, May 26, 1933," in U.S Senate, Subcommittee of the Committee on Education and Labor, *Violations of Free Speech and Rights of Labor,* 75th Cong., 1st sess. (1937), pt. 17, 7561; "Address of the Chairman," American Iron and Steel Institute, *Yearbook* (1933).

10. The authoritative account is Howard M. Gitelman, *Legacy of the Ludlow Massacre: A Chapter in American Labor Relations* (Philadelphia, 1988).

11. This was part of the founding statement of the Special Conference Committee, which began in 1919 for purposes of coordinating and information-sharing on labor matters by ten of the largest and most progressive employers in the country. Young sat on it first as the representative of International Harvester and then, by special dispensation, on behalf of the Industrial Relations Counselors. The statement appears in at least three speeches (Sept. 24, 1935, May 25, 1939, and March 11, 1941). A. H. Young Papers, California Institute of Technology Archives (copies in possession of author).

12. Toni Gilpin, "Left by Themselves: A History of the United Farm Equipment and Metal Workers Union," Ph.D. diss., Yale University, 1992, 66–67, which also includes a careful analysis of the early history of the International Harvester works council plan in chapter 1.

13. I am following the assessment in Daniel Nelson, "The Company Union Movement: A Reexamination," *Business History Review* 56 (Autumn 1982): 335–57.

14. Talk by A. H. Young, Town Hall—Section on Industrial Relations, May 18, 1938, A. H. Young Papers, California Institute of Technology Archives.

15. For a legislative proposal based directly on the ERP steel experience, see Raymond L. Hogler, "Worker Participation, Employer Anti-Unionism, and Labor Law: The Case of the Steel Industry, 1918–1937," *Hofstra Labor Journal* 7 (Fall 1989): 1–69.

16. Leo Troy, "Local Independent Unions and the American Labor Movement," *Industrial and Labor Relations Review* 14 (April 1961): 331–49.

17. For example, "Reckoning with Company Unions: The Case of Thompson Products, 1934–64," *Industrial and Labor Relations Review* 43 (Oct. 1989): 19–40.

18. There is a convenient summary of the Johnson-Richberg plan in Leverett S. Lyon, *The National Recovery Administration: An Analysis and Appraisal* (Washington, 1935), 461–66.

19. Sidney Fine, *The Automobile under the Blue Eagle* (Ann Arbor, 1963), 222–24 and passim for a detailed account.

20. For example, "Meeting of the Automobile Labor Board with the Bargaining Agency Elected by Employees of Cadillac Motor Company, January 3, 1935," NRA Papers, RG 9, box 2, National Archives. In the view of the ALB, the auto settlement required the employer to meet with the bargaining agency but everything beyond that was strictly voluntary. It was expected that the actual development of collective bargaining would be a long-term voluntary process.

21. Quoted in Fine, *The Automobile under the Blue Eagle,* 224–25. On FDR's commitment to the auto settlement as the basic definition of 7(a) rights, see the quotation in Irving Bernstein, *The Turbulent Years: A History of the American Worker, 1933–41* (Boston, 1970), 191.

22. On the legal history, see Irving Bernstein, *The New Deal Collective Bargaining Policy* (Berkeley, 1950), 18–22. On the potency of the company-domination principle, see especially the grudging testimony of James A. Emery, general counsel of the National Association of Manufacturers, in *Legislative History of the National Labor Relations Act, 1935*, 2 vols. (Washington, 1959, repr. 1985), 1:379–81.

23. The early drafts, beginning with the first of January 31, 1934, are reprinted, with commentary, in Kenneth Casebeer, "Drafting Wagner's Act: Leon Keyserling and the Precommittee Drafts of the Labor Disputes Act and the National Labor Relations Act," *Industrial Relations Law Journal* 11 (1989): 73–131.

24. William L. Leiserson to Wagner, March 8, 1934, folder 14, box 1, Leon Keyserling Papers, Georgetown University; Edwin E. Witte, "Hearings on S. 2926," in *Legislative History of the National Labor Relations Act, 1935*, 2 vols. (Washington, 1959, repr. 1985), 1:271–73; James A. Gross, *The Making of the National Labor Relations Board* (Albany, 1974), 68. The successive drafts of the Labor Disputes bill incorporate Leiserson's and Witte's suggestions but are denoted "Confidential Committee Print" and seem not to have been formally added to the March 1 version. They are not reported in the *Legislative History* but can be found in folder 20, box 1, of the Keyserling Papers.

25. The Walsh bill is reprinted in *Legislative History*, 1:1084ff., with Walsh's explanation on 1101ff. One change, not especially noted at the time but of peculiar relevance today, was the deletion from the definition of "employee" (Sec.3 [3] of the Labor Disputes bill) of a proviso stating that strike replacements were not employees; the deletion survived in the drafting of the final Wagner Act.

26. Town Hall Speech, May 28, 1938, A. H. Young Papers, California Institute of Technology Archives.

27. A. H. Young to L. H. Corndorf, June 16, 1934, in *Legislative History*, 2:2225.

28. Leon Keyserling, undated memo [1935], folder 9, box 1, Leon Keyserling Papers, Georgetown University.

29. "Comparison of S. 2926 and S. 1958," *Legislative History*, 1:1320, 1347.

30. In the following discussion I am drawing on my "Workplace Contractualism in Comparative Perspective," in *Industrial Democracy in America: The Ambiguous Promise*, ed. Nelson Lichtenstein and Howell John Harris (New York, 1993), 176–205.

31. Mark Barenberg. "The Political Economy of the Wagner Act: Power, Symbol, and Workplace Cooperation," *Harvard Law Review* 106 (1993): 1379–496.

32. Barry Bluestone and Irving Bluestone, *Negotiating the Future: A Labor Perspective on American Business* (New York, 1992).

5 World War I and Industrial Democracy; or, Why We Have No Works Councils in America

*The occasion for the preceding essay was a conference orga-
nized by Cornell University and the AFL-CIO to explore the issues of
labor law reform then under consideration by the Commission on the
Future of Worker-Management Relations. In advance of publication, the
papers were circulated among the commission members. The chair, John
T. Dunlop, read mine and on that basis invited me to testify before the
commission, although he was unimpressed by my initial foray. There
was, Dunlop suggested, more to my subject than the pre–Wagner Act
events that I had covered in my paper. Dunlop was aware that employee representation plans (ERPs) and works councils had figured promi-
nently in the progressive industrial relations of the 1920s. If we went
back before the New Deal, mightn't light be shed on the commission's
exploration of workplace alternatives to collective bargaining?*

*In my testimony I attempted as best I could to satisfy Dunlop's cu-
riosity. But in truth I was not satisfied with the account I had been able
to offer. I kept returning to Dunlop's complaint that there was more to
the banning of shop committees than the immediate prehistory of the*

This essay originally appeared as "Why No Shop Committees in America: A Narrative History," in *Industrial Relations* 40 (July 2001): 356–76. Reprinted with the permission of Blackwell Publishing Ltd.

Wagner Act. What had been the nation's experience with works coun-
cils? Why the unremitting animosity of the trade unions, so critical not
only in 1935 but also to the frustration of Dunlop's reform efforts six-
ty years later? His queries gave rise to a larger question. Had there ever
been a time when the nation might have opted for a different course?
In the following essay, written for an issue of Industrial Relations *hon-*
oring a pioneering scholar in the field, George Strauss, I offered my
answer.

In this story everything begins with World War I. The cornerstone of wartime labor policy, it turns out, was the shop committee. This was the case
because the shop committee resolved an otherwise intractable dilemma
for the Wilson administration. It was essential to the war effort that labor
and capital be onboard. They made conflicting demands, however. The
price of wartime cooperation by the labor movement was public protection of the right of workers to organize. The price of cooperation by nonunion employers was maintenance of the open shop. These two positions
were not wholly incompatible, because, in principle at any rate, the open
shop did not discriminate against union members but only—as the safe-
guard of the liberty of nonunion workers—stood against recognizing or
dealing contractually with trade unions. It was possible to buy one's way
out of this dilemma, which was what contractors had done in the summer
of 1917, by guaranteeing union standards in lieu of recognition at the military cantonments they were building. The shop committee, however, was
a more elegant solution, cutting as it did right to the core of the dilemma:
Workers had a voice but not union representation.

The shop committee was first proposed by the U.S. Emergency Fleet
Corporation in response to a threatened strike in the Northwest shipyards
in November 1917 and then adopted by other industrial agencies as labor
unrest erupted across the wartime economy. With the creation of the
National War Labor Board (NWLB) in April 1918, the shop committee
became official policy. In implementing this policy, the NWLB fashioned
a body of rules that called, among other things, for federal supervision of
elections; balloting off company premises (despite employer objections);
and plantwide jurisdictions (despite objections by craft unions). But there
was no general mandate. The NWLB acted on a case-by-case basis where
labor disputes threatened war production, so that, aside from certain industries like railroads and mining that came under broad federal administration, shop elections had been held at only about 125 firms by the Armistice, although these included some of the nation's biggest employers.

The shop committee was not, however, exclusively an artifact of wartime. Its immediate roots can be traced to the late Progressive Era, at the confluence of scientific management and industrial democracy. Although it had a long pedigree, industrial democracy became a rallying cry only when reformers hailed it as the antidote to the endemic labor strife brought home to the nation by the McNamaras' dynamiting of the *Los Angeles Times* in 1910.[1] This was the message advanced, most notably, by the U.S. Commission of Industrial Relations (1913–15), whose feisty chief, Frank P. Walsh, went on during the war to become NWLB co-chair. "Industrial democracy" was, of course, an elastic term, and for many progressives, aware of labor's growing prominence in Democratic politics (and Wilson's reelection in 1916), it mainly meant the right to organize and bargain collectively. But that was not, even among labor's partisans, its only meaning.

Especially for Taylorist progressives whose aim it was to democratize scientific management, industrial democracy started on the shop floor. Charles E. Piez, for one, experimented with shop committees at the Link-Belt Company before the war in an effort to "harmonize Scientific Management and Trade Unionism." It was this same Piez who, as head of the Emergency Fleet Corporation, instituted the first wartime shop committees in the Northwest shipyards.[2] Piez belonged to a small circle of labor experts, most of them members of the Taylor Society, who had been thinking about shop committees and suddenly found themselves positioned to put their ideas into practice.

The war itself invested industrial democracy with immensely greater resonance. It became the apotheosis on the home front of the Wilsonian struggle to make the world safe for democracy, and so, more concretely, did the picture of workers voting for their own representatives at the workplace. At that moment the shop committee seemed so deeply implanted, remarked another of its progessive proponents, Louis B. Wehle, "as hardly to seem eradicable."[3]

The shop committee was the handiwork primarily of strategically placed operatives like Piez and Wehle who had migrated to wartime Washington with big ideas about American labor relations. It did not take much to bring organized labor on board, however, which was, for example, Franklin D. Roosevelt's mission as assistant secretary of the navy when he attended the AFL convention after the Emergency Fleet Corporation's 1917 directive for the Northwest shipyards. In fact, Samuel Gompers, in conjunction with that canny wartime bureaucrat-progressive Felix Frankfurter, had already broached the idea before the advisory commission of the Council of National Defense.[4]

Gompers cited as his model the Whitley councils just then being established in Great Britain. Gompers' primary interest in Whitley councils may have been to promote the case he was making for joint labor/management participation in the agencies of war administration. But the Whitley scheme also called for works committees. It did so because neighborhood-based trade unions in Britain did not reach into the workplace (leaving the field to a radical shop-stewards' movement that the wartime government was desperate to rein in). In America that was not the case. In fact, where craft unions were strong, as in some shipyards, wartime shop committees got short shrift.[5] Indeed, the AFL's official endorsement was decidedly ambivalent, predicated on "the basic principle" that workers had the right to organize and the conviction that although shop committees mattered, collective bargaining was "the foundation of all effective [and] just labor administration."[6]

What overrode labor's doubts was a gap different from Britain's—not in the trade-union structure but in the absence of trade unions from so much of American industry. War created the opportunity to make up that deficit, sparking the surging union activity that threatened military production. It quickly became clear that the shop committee could be made to work for unions, whose slates swept NWLB-supervised elections everywhere. The shop committee became, de facto, a union vehicle or, from the jaundiced perspective of employers, "mere camouflage" for the closed shop.[7]

It was not to be expected, of course, that they would roll over and play dead. The more truculent among them resisted NWLB intervention, preferring in a few instances, as with the arms manufacturer Smith and Wesson, government seizure to compliance. Better, however, to beat the board to the punch. A new weapon, peculiarly well adapted to that purpose, had come to hand. This was the employee representation plan which John D. Rockefeller Jr. had been earnestly promoting ever since a bloody strike at the coal mines of his Colorado Fuel and Iron Company in 1914 had exposed him to searing public scrutiny. How many converts Rockefeller might have made in the normal course of events is anybody's guess—not many if we are to go by the initial response—but during the war his scheme seemed like a gift from heaven to embattled open-shop industry.

On its face, the Rockefeller plan, by providing for shop-floor elections, gave workers just what the NWLB's shop committees did but in a manner more to the liking of employers. Rockefeller's particular innovation, distinguishing his plan from earlier schemes, was that it called for *joint* councils, effectively giving management veto rights and simultaneously discouraging any independent voice by the workers' representatives. This was in the long run. The immediate attraction was that the employer stage-managed the entire affair, initiating the plan, overseeing the nominations and balloting, and creating the right atmosphere. Many smaller firms, of course, took preemptive action on their own, making sure (as one employer association advised) "that the committee is of your best employees and not a committee appointed by outside agencies."[8] But big, visible employers could not afford a seat-of-the-pants operation. Rockefeller's Canadian adviser W. L. Mackenzie King, the real brains behind the plan, was soon moving around the country dispensing advice to Bethlehem Steel, General Electric, Youngstown Sheet and Tube, and International Harvester.

In the midst of all this the Armistice suddenly arrived and with it an abrupt end to the nation's shop committee experiment—or rather, to the state's role in that experiment. The reasons for its precipitous retreat are complex, in part reflective of a larger reaction against wartime controls and in part a failure of nerve by a Wilson administration gambling everything on the peacemaking in Paris. In the case of labor policy, moreover, at least formal assent by the parties had always been part of the equation. Thus the NWLB was constituted equally of employer members (chosen by the National Industrial Conference Board) and labor members (chosen by the AFL), with co-chairs selected by each side.

It was something of a miracle, in fact, that the board worked as effectively as it did, due in no small measure to the industry co-chair, William Howard Taft, who, despite his antiunion record on the bench, astonished everyone by robustly defending labor's wartime rights. But the industry side, restive even before the Armistice, was now bent on sabotaging the board. The labor co-chair, Frank P. Walsh, made one desperate effort to save it. He proposed that the huge backlog of cases be settled by the automatic establishment of shop committees, with the board transforming itself into a court of appeals to resolve disputes. Then, when industry members voted him down, he resigned. In any event, the NWLB no longer had the power to enforce even the decisions it had made. As employer defiance stiffened, the board subsided into impotence and soon dissolved.

But employee representation, embraced in wartime to forestall state-mandated shop committees, developed in the turbulent aftermath a momentum of its own. Consider, for example, this riff by Cyrus H. McCormick Jr. at a meeting of International Harvester executives and plant managers on February 25, 1919, debating the merits of the Rockefeller plan:

Our country is just coming out of this great war in which democracy has been fighting autocracy. The working man naturally thinks of the autocracy of the employers and believes that he himself is on the side of democracy. I believe the vote of the working men on many of these things, well controlled by the machinery which this plan will put into effect, will give us a chance to exercise democracy in industry, and that it is one of the things which is bound to come—this recognition, so far as possible, of the working men.[9]

Five weeks later, on April 2, 1919, McCormick attended a select dinner of business leaders at the Metropolitan Club in New York City to hear a report on the labor situation in Britain. The message was that unionization might be the only alternative to Bolshevism. Indeed, as one speaker just back from Paris warned, President Wilson might well return from the peace conference demanding as much from American industry. The audience of magnates bristled, of course, coming forth with a statement for their future guidance: "Reasons Why the Joint Conference Plan of Industrial Employees' Representation Is Better Adapted to American Industrial Conditions Than the So-Called Whitley or National Industrial Conference Plan of England [which assumed union participation]."

Reporting back to his superiors at DuPont, Vice President H. Fletcher Brown urged that the conference's advice be taken that all corporations set up representation plans "as the first and most important step in safeguarding their own interests by securing a loyal, contented and efficient group of employees." Clarence J. Hicks, Rockefeller's resident expert, had already been recruited, and the groundwork was being laid for that reclusive consortium of open-shop giants, the Special Conference Committee.[10]

The next day, May 17, 1919, Fletcher Brown had on his desk a confidential report from the chief of DuPont's Service Department on how the representation plan Hicks had installed at Standard Oil's Bayonne refinery was faring:

> This, clearly, is not industrial democracy. It is instead clever humbug. In the last analysis, it is rather a cumbersome scheme to insure to each employee an opportunity to have his grievances aired and to have them satisfactorily adjusted, provided such adjustment does not involve the expenditure of money by the Company. In any case, the absolute veto power rests with the Company. On the other hand, I have no doubt that the employee thinks he is [acquiring] a voice in management and that the operation of the whole scheme promotes cordial relations between employer and employee. As practiced at Bayonne, the scheme is entirely inocuous [sic] insofar as danger to the Company's established labor policies is concerned.[11]

In following this particular thread of employer thinking I am trying to capture something of the fluidity still infusing the shop committee question after the war. The role of the state might be settled but not yet the place that workplace structures of representation might have in American labor relations. Employers themselves were unsure. The more advanced among them, like Cyrus McCormick, accepted the fact that the "autocratic" methods of the past had to give way to "democracy in industry" but "well controlled by the machinery which this [Rockefeller] plan will put into effect." But how independent a voice would be afforded to (or seized by) workers? And what if they demanded union representation?

Employers could not be certain of the future or, their cautionary words notwithstanding, even their own convictions at this moment of unparalleled crisis. This is why we cannot read the meaning of "clever humbug" in the DuPont man's report on the Bayonne plan. Is he admiring Standard Oil's skill at hoodwinking its employees, or is he deploring its cynicism in denying them real "industrial democracy"?

Management's uncertainties were mirrored by labor's. The antiunion impulses behind the representation plans labor leaders understood all too well, even without being privy to the agitated dinner conversations at the budding Special Conference Committee. But in early 1919 they could not be sure, any more than could management, where employee representation might lead. As the Bureau of Industrial Research noted after a survey of eighteen major firms, works councils were "still unproved and tentative," and their "relation to the spontaneously democratic activities of organized labor [was] still unsettled."[12]

Rockefeller himself spoke in the language of accommodation. Everything society had recently experienced, he asserted in a widely publicized speech after the Armistice, "point[ed] toward the need of more adequate representation of labor in the conduct of industry and the importance of closer relations between labor and capital." Workers had the right to associate, and it was "just as proper and advantageous" for them to form labor unions as for employers to form trade associations. Rockefeller added, however, for the "large proportion" of unorganized workers lacking the benefits of collective bargaining, the workplace offered an alternative arena for representation. Rockefeller cited as promising precedents the NWLB shop committees and Whitley councils. What he was proposing was a "simpler" plan, "building from the bottom up." It would start with individual plants but be capable of infinite expansion and take as its central concerns conditions at work, individual grievances, "good will," and "community spirit." This was "a method of representation which is just, which is effective, which is applicable to all employees whether organized or not" and "which does not compete or interfere with organizations or associations in existence."[13]

Meeting with him soon after, Gompers did not take exception to Rockefeller's formulation and, indeed, later assured Rockefeller that his words deserved wide distribution among working people. Gompers' private thoughts must have been much like those of his wartime ally Felix Frankfurter's, that "Mr. Rockefeller's 'creed' undoubtedly looks in the right direction," but that the emphasis was misplaced and "must be upon . . . a ready recognition of labor's independent responsibility in working out the problems . . . and not the concession made by management, however wholeheartedly made or generously conceived."[14]

These meetings with Gompers were no aberration. Rockefeller had been courting union leaders ever since the Colorado coal strike sparked his enthusiasm for employee representation. Stung by charges of antiunionism, he had met with the national officers of the United Mine Workers in 1915 and arrived at an understanding by which they withdrew the demand for union recognition while he authorized negotiations for a contract directly with employees at the Colorado and Iron Company through the representation plan, including a provision against discrimination for union membership (and help in quashing indictments against the strike leaders). Left hanging was what might happen if CF&I miners opted for the union. The UMWA adopted a wait-and-see attitude; in Colorado its leaders spoke favorably of the Rockefeller plan.

During the war Rockefeller formed warm ties with Gompers. Afterward, he helped finance an impressive bust in Gompers' honor and, several years later, Gompers' autobiography, *Seventy Years of Life and Labor* (1924). There were also discussions about funding an AFL propaganda campaign to counter Bolshevism among American workers. Moreover, Rockefeller's two closest advisers, Mackenzie King and Raymond B. Fosdick (later of the Rockefeller Foundation), were decidedly pro-union, although they trimmed their advice to what they thought the master could bear. Emboldened by the postwar turmoil, both in early 1919 pressed him to be more forthright about granting union recognition at Rockefeller properties. King even developed a plan for the coexistence of collective bargaining and employee representation, suggesting that at a substantially organized refinery of Standard Oil of Indiana the unions be consulted about the plan's introduction and given seats on all joint committees and that the latter's functions be limited to such noncontractual matters as sanitation, safety, and labor-management cooperation.

Faced by a real choice, Rockefeller said no. For all his friendly words he had deeply ambivalent feelings about organized labor. Howard Gitelman mulls over this problem at length in his authoritative book on Rockefeller (which I am following here) and concludes that the millionaire never made up his mind. He wanted to be believe that he—and his plan—were not antiunion, but union recognition he could not bring himself to accept.

To his credit, however, Rockefeller was not deceived about what was at stake in his dilemma. Powerful employers like himself might create employee representation, but no amount of power could command its success. It was not even a question of how well individual plans might work in practice. By what standard? With what credibility? The answers might have come, as in wartime, from the state. But with the state's withdrawal that role fell, by default, to the labor movement. With labor's assent, employee representation might have multiplied, as Rockefeller's post-Armistice manifesto had envisioned; found a modus vivendi with collective bargaining; and recast the American industrial landscape. With labor against it, employee representation would always be suspect, always in the realm of "clever humbug." Thus Rockefeller's delight at his understanding with the United Mine Workers over the Colorado plan, which "'had taken the fangs out of' the one thing we had to fear, namely, that the union would say that the agreement made with the employees was a substitute for unionism."[15] In early 1919 the labor movement still hesitated and then did just what Rockefeller had so feared.

———————

At the June convention the AFL took its stand against employee representation, defined specifically as "systems of collective bargaining akin to the Rockefeller plan." The resolution it adopted contained an incisive critique and an uncompromising conclusion. These plans—by now firmly designated as "company unions"—were "a snare and delusion," and unionists should "have nothing to do with them." The AFL demanded "the right of collective bargaining through the only kind of organization fitted for this purpose—the trade-union."

The resolution's sponsor was the National Committee for Organizing Iron and Steel Workers. This is a fact of cardinal importance, signifying the moment of confluence between workplace representation and a great struggle for collective bargaining. The standard account of that struggle is my *Labor in Crisis: The Steel Strike of 1919* (1965), written, as I remarked at its reissue in 1987, "from the vantage point of triumphant industrial unionism during the New Deal."[16] Now that the vantage point is not CIO triumph but, one might say, its wreckage, we can extract from *Labor in Crisis* an embedded thread, one that meant so little at the time that I did not mention the AFL resolution condemning company unionism. In what follows I am returning to my old work, in effect reclaiming and developing more fully a story I had forgotten I knew about how the steel strike of 1919 determined the American fate of workplace representation.

In the early twentieth century the steel industry stood as the great American bastion of the open shop. The industry was a formidable opponent—highly concentrated, well financed, boastful of its welfarist programs, and implacably against collective bargaining. The labor movement was hard put to respond, hobbled as it was by a craft structure at odds with the industry's continuous-flow technology and by nativist disdain for the mass of immigrant workers laboring twelve-hour days in the mills. Only late in the war did the AFL bestir itself, prompted by its unexpected triumph in meatpacking—another archetypal mass-production industry—to establish on August 1, 1918, the National Committee for Organizing Iron and Steel Workers.

The National Committee was skimpily financed, but its director, William Z. Foster, fresh from the meatpacking drive, was the best in the business. Foster had only enough funds for the Chicago district, but quick success there enabled the drive to move on to other steel centers and begin the assault on the industry's core around Pittsburgh. "Beyond all question the steel industry is being organized," Foster reported on January 4, 1919.[17] By now, however, with the war over, the campaign would have to proceed in the teeth of employer opposition.

Steel happened to be an industry in which, even before the national drive, the Rockefeller plan had made considerable inroads. The most militant, and most strategically placed, war workers were the metal crafts in arms-producing factories—Remington, Smith and Wesson, General Electric, Midvale Steel and Ordnance, and Bethlehem. The last two also operated basic steel plants and were, in fact, the largest independents in the industry. Both had been hit by machinists' strikes in the spring of 1918, and, like other firms threatened by NWLB intervention, both had invoked Rockefeller's representation plan. Bethlehem's clumsy maneuvers failed, however, and it grudgingly accepted NWLB-supervised elections at its main South Bethlehem works. Midvale, more nimble, fended off the NWLB and installed a representation plan, which in early 1919 won a stamp of approval from the expiring NWLB.[18]

The key figure at Midvale was its vice president, William B. Dickson, the industry's maverick, famous before the war for championing the eight-hour day and known even to ruminate about collective bargaining. The wartime crisis ignited Dickson's ruminations into flaming advocacy of "industrial democracy," although, like Rockefeller, he stopped just short of union recognition. Despite his zeal, Dickson failed to persuade Judge Elbert H. Gary, the old-line head of U.S. Steel, the dominant company in the industry. Gary regarded employee representation as a rebuke to his stewardship and a first step to unionization. But among the independents the roster of the converted was impressive—besides Midvale, Bethlehem (in plants not covered by the NWLB order), Youngstown Sheet and Tube, Inland, Lukens, Wisconsin Steel (an International Harvester subsidiary), and, earliest of all, the Pueblo steel plant of Rockefeller's Colorado Fuel and Iron Company.

The steel drive first encountered employee representation in a big way at Midvale's giant Cambria works in Johnstown, Pennsylvania. Despite their skepticism, organizers decided—in the words of George Soule, who investigated Johnstown for the Interchurch World Movement—"to give it a fair trial by campaigning for and electing as representatives, union members who would demand the eight-hour day."[19] A number did win in the January 1919 balloting only to be fired wholesale along with hundreds of other unionists the next month when the company cut back sharply on production. In preparation for a showdown, plant officials began to stockpile rifles and deputize loyal employees. The National Committee, plunged into its first real crisis, appealed to Washington for help. Dickson was, in fact, shocked by these events and bitterly angry at his colleagues—"all Bourbon reactionaries" as he called them. He had the hard-line plant manager fired, rescinded strike preparations, and pledged that unionists would not be discriminated against. To no avail. There would be no reinstatements and, because the company insisted it would deal only with employee representatives, no reason for anything but animus against the plan.

The Cambria debacle only crystallized things, however. Whatever they might have made of the scheme at other times, when the organizing drive swept them up steelworkers everywhere scorned employee representation. Thus, at a rank-and-file steel conference in Pittsburgh on May 26 intended to air grievances, the company unions were excoriated from the floor—the upshot being, a few weeks later, the National Committee resolution at the AFL convention. The committee's key operative, William Z. Foster, had initially taken a cautious line, suggesting in fact that "trade unions [could] function in connection with shop committees" if employers refused to deal with outside officials.[20] But once rank-and-file sentiment hardened, Foster shifted ground. A veteran syndicalist, he could have regarded employee representation only as an impediment to the class struggle he was seeking to advance by working inside the AFL.

Most likely, the virile language and marshaled arguments of the AFL resolution were Foster's, and he may even have instigated it. But there was no conspiracy in that resolution. The repudiation of employee representation was an imperative of the organizing drive itself.

The proof was in the turnout when the great strike started on September 22, 1919. How the ERPs had actually performed seemed hardly to matter. At Cambria after the union presence ended, the plan turned farcical, treated mainly as a soft touch by its elected representatives, many of them foremen. They rewarded the company at a cushy Atlantic City conference in August 1919 by denouncing wage increases and proposing harder work as a remedy for the high cost of living. The Cambria plant was closed for two months by the strike. At International Harvester's Wisconsin works, on the other hand, the employee representatives, led by the unionists among them, stood up against management in demanding a basic eight-hour day, which, on appeal to him, the company's president Harold McCormick unexpectedly granted. The Wisconsin works also shut down on September 22. (The emasculation of the works council came afterward, when it became a court presiding over the rehire of individual strikers.) Even at Bethlehem, where the shop committee system of wartime still survived, workers overrode the advice of the leadership and joined the strike after a week, demanding full union recognition.[21]

It was not the strike itself, however, but the desperate efforts to end it that finally settled the question of employee representation. The occasion was a National Industrial Conference, called into being by President Wilson to forge a labor policy for the postwar era. There was nothing exceptionable about Wilson's initiative; Canada and Britain were holding similar conclaves. But in the American case these deliberations, which began on October 6, 1919, took place while the greatest strike for recognition in the country's history raged.

The labor delegation, regarding the Industrial Conference as the only hope for the steel strike, immediately proposed that an arbitration committee be appointed, pending whose decision the steelworkers would go back to work. A second resolution asserted, among other principles, the right of wage-earners to organize and bargain collectively, which was, of course, the core issue in the strike. The employer and public delegates had little stomach for intervening, and, given that any action required a majority vote by all three delegations, the conference would certainly not do so without the assent of the steel industry, which Judge Gary, a public delegate, finally declined to give. In the meantime, a great debate over the meaning of labor's rights had taken center stage.

The debate began with a demand by the public delegation that the open shop—"the right of any wage earner to refrain from joining any organization or to deal directly with his employer if he so chooses"—be endorsed. The labor group swallowed hard and agreed in exchange for explicit recognition of "the right of wage earners to organize in trade and labor unions, to bargain collectively, to be represented by representatives of their own choosing."[22] Initially, the public delegation accepted this formulation; indeed, Rockefeller (like Gary a public member) spoke in its favor. But his remarks, echoing his post-Armistice address, invoked the principle of employee representation, and that at once became the litmus test of labor's resolution. Did it include the right of workers to be represented by employee representatives? On this point the labor delegates were conflicted. Their natural bent as trade unionists was to think that only trade unions legitimately represented workers and, with Gompers briefly sidelined by illness, that's what they said.[23] The public group thereupon substituted "associations of their own choosing" for "trade and labor unions" or, as a concession, adding "and other associations" to the latter phrase.

The Industrial Conference nearly broke up at this point, but Gompers had been angling all along for some middle ground. When the stricken President Wilson from his sickbed issued a last-minute appeal, the labor delegation offered a final compromise that satisfied the public group: "The right of wage earners to organize without discrimination, to bargain collectively, to be represented by representatives of their own choosing in negotiations and adjustments with their employers in respect to wages, hours of labor, and the relations and conditions of employment, is recognized."[24]

We need to pause here to take in the significance of this statement. As regards self-organization, all that was new was the suggestion that its exercise be respected or, possibly, legally protected. "Representatives of their own choosing" was something else. It implied a more or less formal process for choice by workers, standards assuring the integrity of the procedure, and, overseeing it, an external, probably state-empowered agency. Given the preceding debate, moreover, what was contemplated would be a real systemic choice, with employee representation just as valid as trade unionism. At a less fraught moment union leaders might have drawn back from a proposition so at odds with labor's self-definition as a voluntaristic movement organically linked to the working class. But in 1919, when everything they had won in wartime was at stake, employee choice offered a level playing field with a prize they seemed incapable of collecting by their own power: union recognition. Understanding that, the employer delegation rejected labor's resolution. They conceded the right to organize and bargain collectively—a mark in itself, of course, of how far the ideological ground had shifted—but that only hardened their resolve.

In a close reading of the debate, Haggai Hurvitz finds an uncompromising indictment being forged, with trade unionism cast in the grimmest light, driven not by any genuine interest in uplifting workers but only by the ambitions of union bosses. It followed that employers had to stand fast on the question of union recognition—to insist, in fact, that their freedom of choice was the "correlative right" of labor's freedom of association: "No employer should be required to deal with labor unions." Workers' rights would be fully satisfied by choosing representatives "from their own number."[25]

It was a near thing. Despite elaborate precautions by the lead National Industrial Conference Board, the employer delegation almost gave way (splitting ten to seven) and would have done so, administration figures were convinced, but for the steel strike.[26] Of course, rescuing the strike was the whole point so far as labor was concerned. With employer rejection of Gompers' resolution, the union delegation walked out, and the President's Industrial Conference collapsed.

The coda to this story begins with Herbert Hoover. Back from his celebrated labors on behalf of European war victims, he was tapped to serve as vice chair of the successor to the failed Industrial Conference, this time limited to public members. Hoover was a great believer in shop committees, both for restoring personal contact in the modern workplace and for eliminating "waste" in industry that was this engineer's true obsession. Under Hoover's guidance, the President's Second Industrial Conference proposed that democratic workplace representation be made the foundation of the nation's labor practice. The resolution of industrial conflict "must come from the bottom, not the top" and must arise from "deliberate organization" of the relations between workers and employers at the shop level. Hoover acknowledged that labor leaders had cause to regard "shop representation as a subtle weapon directed against the union," but plans so conceived would never be "a lasting agency of industrial peace." The relationship ought to be "complementary," not "mutually exclusive," with unions bargaining over the contractual terms of employment while shop committees devoted themselves to local grievances, production problems and, more broadly, "whatever subjects the representatives come to feel as having a relation to their work."[27] Hoover was advancing nothing less than an American version of the works-council system emerging at this time in Europe, only by means of voluntary action rather than state policy.[28]

When he took his program on the road, Hoover ran into a brick wall. At a private meeting with leading industrialists—the known list suggests the Special Conference Committee—Hoover urged the assemblage, if it wanted an era of stability and progress, to embrace collective bargaining and establish relations with the AFL. No minutes of this meeting survive, but years later one participant (Cyrus S. Ching) reminded Hoover that his "idea got a very cold reception."[29]

So Hoover turned to organized labor. At an extraordinary session with the AFL Executive Council he made his pitch for a "new economic system" based on ever-rising productivity. If the labor movement in league with the engineers committed itself to efficiency, employers would be compelled to join the partnership. Everything depended, however, on new forms of "cooperation between management and worker" and, on labor's part, "an acceptance of certain principles of shop councils."[30] There was much in this that trade unionists liked; labor-management cooperation, in fact, became a favorite AFL theme in the 1920s. But they were immovably against employee representation. The condemnation they had already leveled against Hoover's Industrial Conference—that it gave "encouragement and permanency to the various forms of company unions and shop organizations and various forms of so-called employee representation, whose chief merit is that they serve the purposes of the employers by organizing the workers away from each other"—voiced an iron opposition that, once fixed in 1919, became permanent and as implacable in John Dunlop's day as in Herbert Hoover's.[31]

A decade and a half later the Wagner Act declared company domination of labor organizations unlawful in language so sweeping that it effectively proscribed workplace forms of representation, including Hoover's shop committees. Historians have not tracked this astonishing outcome back to the crisis of 1919 because the trail turned cold in the 1920s. Employee representation persisted—1.5 million workers were covered at the end of the decade—but not the debate over industrial democracy that had animated it.

As the union threat receded, employee representation came to be valued by its advocates primarily as an asset in progressive labor relations. This was, to be sure, not new. It was employee motivation that had originally fueled the Taylorist interest in shop committees, and "the Personal

Relation in Industry" (to use the title of his stock prewar speech) had been Rockefeller's main theme as an evangelist for his Colorado plan.[32]

In the 1920s this labor-relations emphasis revived mightily. For the New Era's lead industrial firms, employee representation became emblematic of best practice under the aegis of advanced personnel management. Thus Bethlehem Steel's chair, Charles M. Schwab, capitalism's advocate of industrial democracy in 1918, ten years later was extolling the operational benefits of employee representation: "increased efficiency, elimination of waste, and improved methods" and "a growth in morale and in sympathy and understanding between employees and officials." What firms most valued, reported the National Industrial Conference Board, was the "welding together [of] management and working force into a single, cohesive productive unit."[33] Whether employee representation was an exercise in industrial democracy became quite beside the point in the triumphant age of welfare capitalism.

Not, however, on the railroads. There, the battle for collective bargaining raged on; management made unabashed use of company unions to uproot the nonoperating crafts; and, of critical importance, the federal government did not—could not—bow out. There also, following Ruth O'Brien's illuminating study, we can pick up the doctrinal track where it leaves off in 1919 with the fateful words in labor's declaration of rights at the President's Industrial Conference: "representatives of their own choosing."[34]

The Republican-sponsored Transportation Act of 1920 was unequivocally an antiunion measure, returning railroads to private control (over labor's fervent opposition) and dismantling the wartime arrangements by which the AFL's nonoperating crafts had prospered as exclusive bargaining agents for their classifications. The Transportation Act contemplated not a revived open shop for these classifications, however, but the continuation of collective bargaining, only now "between representatives designated and authorized so to confer by the carriers, or their employees." With those oblique words the principle of employee choice—representatives of their own choosing—first entered the statute books. In the context of the Transportation Act, of course, only the antiunion side hit home. Employee choice was the wedge for dislodging the nonoperating crafts. But once in place employee choice unveiled a confounding logic of its own.

The Railroad Labor Board created by the Transportation Act was weak, endowed with dubious quasi-judicial powers, and stacked against labor. Yet on announcing what the railroads most wanted—termination of the national nonoperating crafts agreements—the board promulgated rules that emphatically protected the right to organize and—precocious notion!—called for majority rule in the determination of bargaining agents.[35] And when the Pennsylvania Railroad, affecting to comply, broke off relations with the AFL crafts and proceeded to hold elections limited to its own employees—in effect, setting up an employee representation plan—the board struck back with unexpected force, voiding the election and condemning Pennsylvania's action as one "which throttles the majority and establishes the representation of a coerced and subservient minority."[36] In *Pennsylvania Railroad v. U.S. Railroad Board* (1923), the Supreme Court upheld the company—it could not be required to comply because the board lacked enforcement powers—but went on to rule unanimously that the board's actions had correctly expressed the law's intent and, moreover, had not violated the railroad's constitutional rights. On the ground, *Pennsylvania's* machinations helped trigger the great shopmen's strike of 1922, a conflict so chastening in its fury that all parties realized that stable labor relations required effective machinery for adjusting disputes and enforcing the rights of railroad workers.

Over the course of this Republican decade, as the principle of free choice began to bite, company unionism lost legal ground until, in the definitive *Texas and New Orleans Railroad v. Railway Clerks* (1930), it was utterly defeated. In this case, the Supreme Court unanimously upheld the disestablishment of a company union on the ground that it violated the provision of the Railway Labor Act (1926) prohibiting "interference, influence or coercion" by the employer in the designation of representatives by employees. The finding of company domination was laid out, in all its essentials, and from there passed intact into the Wagner Act.[37] *Texas and New Orleans*, moreover, opened a constitutional pathway for New Deal labor law. Standing in the way was *Adair v. U.S.* (1908), which had declared that railroads could not be prohibited from discharging employees for union membership because such prohibition violated their liberty of contract under at-will employment.

The focus on company unionism enabled *Texas and New Orleans* to shift the ground from *Adair:* "The statute is not aimed at this right of the employers [to select . . . employees or to discharge them] but at the interference with the right of employees to representatives of their own choosing. As the carriers subject to the act have no constitutional right to interfere with the freedom of the employees in making their selections, they cannot complain of the statute on constitutional grounds."[38] The crucial decision upholding the Wagner Act in 1937, *NLRB v. Jones and Laughlin*, disposed of *Adair* by citing *Texas and New Orleans*.

Between *Texas and New Orleans* and *Jones and Laughlin*, of course, an immense political terrain had to be traversed. Along the way, most certainly, there were junctures at which workplace forms of representation might have been accommodated within the emerging national labor law. At every critical point that possibility was defeated by the unremitting opposition of organized labor and by the invincible antiunionism of American employers. All this is evident in the record of the early New Deal and is set forth in my 1994 essay on the origins of Section 8a(2).[39] What I did not know was how rooted this outcome was in earlier events, how fixed by lines of battle first formed in 1919 and by the cumulative weight of the principle of employee choice brought forth by that postwar crisis.

Notes

1. See, for example, *Industrial Democracy in America: The Ambiguous Legacy*, ed. Nelson Lichtenstein and Howell John Harris (New York, 1992), chs. 1, 2.

2. Joseph A. McCartin, *Labor's Great War: The Struggle for Industrial Democracy and the Origins of Modern Labor Relations* (Chapel Hill, 1997), 79–80.

3. McCartin, *Labor's Great War*, 80.

4. Howard M. Gitelman, *Legacy of the Ludlow Massacre: A Chapter in American Industrial Relations* (Philadelphia, 1988), 224–25.

5. David Montgomery, *The Fall of the House of Labor: The Workplace, the State, and American Labor Activism, 1865–1925* (New York, 1987), 418–19.

6. John R. Commons, ed., *Trade Unions and Labor Problems*, 2d ser. (New York, 1921), 345–46.

7. McCartin, *Labor's Great War*, 103; cf. Jeffrey Haydu, *Making American Industry Safe for Democracy: Comparative Perspectives on the State and Employee Representation in the Era of World War I* (Urbana, 1997).

8. Valerie Jean Connor, *The National War Labor Board: Stability, Social Justice, and the Voluntary State in World War I* (Chapel Hill, 1983), 127–28.

9. "Minutes of Meeting, February 25–26, 1919," 6, folder 213, International Harvester Archives, courtesy of Roland Marchand.

10. Folder of Special Conference Committee documents (copied from various in-house collections), Hagley Library. The key document, "Memorandum, H. F. Brown to Irenee DuPont, May 16, 1919," is summarized with generous excerpts in Raymond L. Hogler and Guillermo J. Grenier, *Employee Participation and Labor Law in the American Workplace* (New York: Quorum Books, 1992), 32–34.

11. William P. Allen to C. A. Patterson (copies to H. F. Brown and others), May 17, 1919, acc. 1662, box 27, DuPont Papers, Hagley Library.

12. Montgomery, *The Fall of the House of Labor*, 411.

13. John D. Rockefeller Jr., "The Human Relation in Industry," *Current Affairs*, Dec. 16, 1918, 7, 42–43.

14. Gitelman, *Legacy of the Ludlow Massacre*, 269–71.

15. Ibid., 171.

16. David Brody, *Labor in Crisis: The Steel Strike of 1919* (1965, repr. Urbana, 1987), 190.

17. Brody, *Labor in Crisis*, 76.

18. Gerald. G. Eggert, *Steelmasters and Labor Reform, 1886–1923* (Pittsburgh, 1981), ch. 5.

19. Eggert, *Steelmasters*, 129.

20. Montgomery, *The Fall of the House of Labor*, 420.

21. Eggert, *Steelmasters*, 126–28; Robert Ozanne, *A Century of Labor-Management Relations at McCormick and International Harvester* (Madison, 1967), 124–26; Brody, *Labor in Crisis*, 112–13.

22. Brody, *Labor in Crisis*, 120.

23. In fact, they were only echoing the AFL's reconstruction program, which had been silent on the shop committee issue and had equated industrial democracy strictly with the "right to organize in trade unions." Montgomery, *The Fall of the House of Labor*, 417–18.

24. Brody, *Labor in Crisis*, 122–23.

25. Haggai Hurvitz, "Ideology and Industrial Conflict: President Wilson's First Industrial Conference of October 1919," *Labor History* 18 (Fall 1977): 522.

26. Hurvitz, "Ideology," 515, 521; Brody, *Labor in Crisis*, 123, 128.

27. Robert H. Zieger, "Herbert Hoover, the Wage-Earner, and the 'New Economic System,' 1919–1929," *Business History Review* 51 (Summer 1977): 165–66; Gary Dean Best, "President Wilson's Second Industrial Conference, 1919–1920," *Labor History* 16 (Fall 1975): 517–18; Charles E. Harvey, "John D. Rockefeller, Jr., Herbert Hoover, and President Wilson's Industrial Conference of 1919–1920," in *Voluntarism, Planning, and the State: The American Planning Experience, 1914–1946*, ed. Jerold E. Brown and Patrick D. Eagan (Westport, 1988), 25–48.

28. James E. Cronin and Carmen Sirianni, eds., *Work, Community, and Power: The Experience of Labor in Europe and America, 1900–1925* (Philadelphia, 1983).

29. Gitelman, *Legacy of the Ludlow Massacre*, 326–27.

30. Zieger, "Herbert Hoover," 171–73.

31. Jean Trepp McKelvey, *AFL Attitudes toward Production, 1900–1932* (Ithaca, 1932), 88–89.

32. John D. Rockefeller, Jr., "The Personal Relation in Industry" (1917), reprinted in *The Management of Workers: Selected Documents*, ed. Leon Stein and Philip Taft (New York, 1971).

33. David Brody, "The Rise and Decline of Welfare Capitalism," in *Workers in Industrial America: Essays on the Twentieth-Century Struggle* (New York, 1980), 56.

34. Ruth O'Brien, *Labor's Paradox: The Republican Origins of New Deal Labor Policy, 1886–1935* (Chapel Hill, 1998).

35. The rules are reproduced in Irving Bernstein, *New Deal Collective Bargaining Policy* (Berkeley, 1950), 20.

36. Leo Troy, "Labor Representation on American Railways," *Labor History* 2 (Fall 1961): 305.

37. "The circumstances of the soliciting of authorizations and memberships on behalf of the Association, the fact that employees of the Railroad Company who

were active in promoting the development of the Association were permitted to devote their time to that enterprise without deduction from their pay, the charge to the Railroad Company of expenses incurred in recruiting members of the Association, the reports made to the Railroad Company of the progress of these efforts, and the discharge from the service of the Railroad Company of leading representatives of the Brotherhood and the cancellation of their passes." 281 U.S. 549 (1930).

38. Ibid.

39. See chapter 4 of this volume.

6   Reforming the
American Workplace?

On one plane, the debate over Section 8a(2) was about politics and law. Here, a labor historian like myself could move with some confidence, mobilizing what he knew to advance the deliberations of the Dunlop Commission. But on another plane the debate was about industrial relations or, as practitioners increasingly preferred it, "human resource management." Here I found the past harder to read, in part, no doubt, because of a lack of expertise on my part, but also because of the ambiguous history of American industrial relations, which is more about the proselytizing discipline than about workplace experience. We know what industrial-relations experts preached but not what actual impact, if any, they had on shop-floor practice. Readers will note the skeptical strain in the three reviews that constitute my slight contribution to the industrial-relations side of the debate over workplace reform. The final entry in this chapter represents an effort at merging the two sides of the debate at what seemed, at the time, a climactic moment.

***

THREE REVIEWS

Barry and Irving Bluestone, *Negotiating the Future:*
A Labor Perspective on American Business (1993)

The past twenty years have been a humbling time for American capitalism. The reversal of fortunes that began in the early 1970s was all the more shocking because it came on the heels of two postwar decades of unparalleled economic performance and because the loss of industrial leadership to the once-despised Japanese seemed so decisive. In their distress, American employers have looked for culprits in many directions. But no candidate seemed likelier than the shop floor, where authoritarian methods of production first conceived by Frederick W. Taylor and Henry Ford stood in glaring contrast to German craftsmanship and Japanese team spirit. Given the market pressures, the politics of the Reagan decade, and the antiunionism always abiding within American industry, labor unions would have been thrown on the defensive, no matter what. But the rallying cry of American "competitiveness" gave a license to union-busting, much as the dogma of the "open shop" did in earlier times.

Embattled unions have responded ambiguously. They have resisted as best they could, but many of them—by no means all—also conceded that the adversarial system, so-called, needed reforming. No labor leader has been more closely identified with joint experiments than Irving Bluestone, pioneer of the Quality of Work Life Program at the United Auto Workers. *Negotiating the Future,* written with his son, the political economist Barry Bluestone, is the ultimate statement of progressive trade unionism today, the most far-reaching exposition of labor's role in the postindustrial economy we have.

For starters, the Bluestones try to shed labor's identification as a special interest. In the current crisis, they say, the movement is committed above all to restoring American competitiveness. Productivity, quality, and innovation are the key words echoing through the book. Why all three have broken down is the subject of a lengthy discussion that concludes, predictably, that the main reason was the nation's failed labor relations. The Bluestones situate the unions at the center of the competitiveness crisis—not as part of the problem but as essential to the solution. They admit that blame for past error lies partly with the unions. But they are far more critical of corporate management, which after World War II made a determined defense of its prerogatives against the claims of a resurgent CIO. Management rights clauses won in that fight dealt a fatal blow to any genuine partnership across the class divide. Employers insisted that everything not specified in the contract was off limits to unions. This covered nearly all decisions regarding investment, products, technology, and pricing. For the Bluestones, elimination of the management rights clause is the sine qua non of future labor relations.

They affirm the trade-union principle that without co-equal power there can be no economic justice. Arbitrary power in the hands of management corrupts even the most sophisticated nonunion employee involvement scheme that human resource consultants can dream up. The power workers gain through union organization, in turn, has to be translated into contractually binding rights. Far from seeking to abolish the contract, the Bluestones see it as the cornerstone on which labor-management partnership must be built.

The union contract of the future gets a new name, however—the Enterprise Compact—which begins with the various forms of workplace participation and gain-sharing already in place but expanded so as to achieve what the Bluestones call "co-management" of the workplace. Audaciously, they move out of the factory to advocate co-management at every level of the firm, up to and including the chief executive's office. Three preconditions govern the Bluestones' proposal: first, that labor commit itself to the goal of a "globally competitive firm"; second, that management commit itself to company growth and market share rather than short-term profit maximization; and, third, that all "stakeholders" share on an equitable and specified basis in the earnings of the firm.

From these preconditions the Bluestones fashion a seven-point compact specifying productivity goals, wage increases, pricing policy, quality, job security, and gain-sharing for workers. Point 7 bears full quotation:

> The company and the union agree that all strategic enterprise decisions will be made through *joint action.* These decisions include, but are not restricted to, product pricing, the purchasing of inputs, marketing and advertising, methods of production, the introduction of new technology, investments in new capital and products, and the subcontracting of production. The existing management-rights clause in the traditional contract shall be deleted.

All of this is not exactly pie in the sky. The Bluestones have a prototype in GM's Saturn project, where work rules and job classifications have been swept aside in favor of a flexible team system, plus a structure of joint councils that gives the union a voice up to the highest levels of the GM subsidiary. For now at least, the Saturn car is a hit, and the project that produced it serves as a source of inspiration for the Enterprise Compact. But it's too early to tell whether Saturn is a genuine breakthrough or only a special case. Better that we take a longer view and consider the Enterprise Compact as an artifact of the current trade-union crisis.

The notion of co-managing the firm is not new, although in earlier incarnations it was called industrial democracy. The moment of origin of industrial democracy lies in the late nineteenth century, when small-scale enterprise gave way to the great vertically integrated firm—and with it the modern concept of management as a distinct function. An ideal of democratized industry inspired progressives for many years and periodically was seized on by trade unionists—the Plumb plan for tripartite operation of the railroads after World War I, the industrial councils advocated by the CIO for running defense industries in the early phases of World War II, and afterward the heady talk (which, except for Walter Reuther's abortive drive to get GM to "open the books," it mostly was) of a labor voice in management.

All these initiatives elicited furious opposition from management, which invariably defined them as fatal to American free enterprise. And where, as after World War II, the threat seemed credible, no price was too high to thwart it, not the costly 1946 strike GM endured as its competitors picked up market share nor afterward the generous contract provisions that paid for the management rights clause.

Why do the Bluestones believe that managerial prerogative no longer commands that unwavering loyalty? It can only be because they sense a drastic loss of confidence by management, as if American capitalism had arrived at the equivalent of perestroika in the former Soviet Union. Measured by performance over the past twenty years, maybe that's how things should be. But clearly they are not. Witness the ever-more inflated salaries commanded by chief executives; the attentive monitoring of their comings and goings on the business pages of the press; and the fact that while college graduates and newly minted engineers, lawyers, and academics languish, 95 percent of this year's graduates of the Harvard Business School have jobs before commencement.

If anything, the new competitiveness puts a premium on the management function and casts the Enterprise Compact in a faintly anachronistic light. The elaborate consultative process it envisages assumes a managerial hierarchy now rapidly being dismantled and a deliberate policymaking pace just as everything is becoming fast-action. And what of irresolvable differences? One possibility, the Bluestones suggest, is leaving the last word to management, not unlike (in a telling simile) the vice president "casting the deciding vote when there is a tie vote" in the U.S. Senate. Alternatively, a mediator might be called in, or the issue be put to third-party arbitration. One can imagine what a hoot these suggestions might give the new chief at IBM, whose first major act was to jettison the firm's celebrated job-security policy and announce that the downsizing he intended—thirty-nine thousand jobs—would take place in one single blow.

Still, it is true that little is heard nowadays about the sanctity of the managerial prerogative. And there on the back cover is a mild endorsement of the Bluestones' book by the president of the National Association of Manufacturers. It may be that corporate distress has drawn unions into the management realm frequently enough to have eroded the dogmatism we once would have heard from such a figure. But his complacency probably derives more from a painful truth about the Enterprise Compact. Demands for industrial democracy have characteristically come at flood-tides of the labor movement. This one comes at its nadir and springs not from labor's sense of power but from the slim hope that it can make a case for acceptance.

At the core of the Bluestones' argument is the claim that failed labor relations are the source of America's economic malaise and that mending the system can only occur in partnership with the unions. To begin with, we don't know for a fact that the first part of that proposition is true. After all, it was under the Ford-Taylor system that labor productivity rose to a historic high of 3 percent a year in the 1950s and 1960s. Nor is it clear, insofar as the sharp decline thereafter can be attributed to that system, that participatory programs are a remedy.

To their credit, the Bluestones take the question seriously and devote a lengthy chapter to research on employee participation, with entirely inconclusive results. They argue that the record of success is stronger in union than nonunion settings because of the inherent advantages of joint administration and shared power. But even here, the quantitative evidence is ambiguous. In the end, they fall back on exemplary cases such as Saturn, which are by definition persuasive. But for every example one can find a counterexample. If the union is crucial at Saturn and GM's innovative plant in Fremont, California, then why have Toyota and Nissan managers—whose work practices serve as models for General Motors—fought so hard against organizing drives by the United Auto Workers? The best the Bluestones can say is that the exemplary cases they discuss show "not so much the current state of success" as "the *potential* of EI [Employee Involvement] if it is implemented properly and effectively."

There is a palpable unreality at the heart of the Bluestones' book. They speak of the need for creating a "benign climate" as if antiunionism was a matter of bad temper. "Old grudges" have to be set aside, they say, and so do "misconceptions" about the rigidity and self-seeking of unions. Antiunionism is not the product of grudges or misconceptions but of cool business calculation. If, as most labor economists now suggest, union workers may be more efficient than nonunion workers, there is no question that unionized firms are less profitable than nonunion firms. The gains in labor productivity do not counterbalance the union wage premium. In effect, unions redistribute the earnings of the firm to the advantage of their members.

Since they well understand this reality, American employers enter collective bargaining out of necessity, rarely by choice. And while they then accommodate themselves as best they can and find benefits in collective bargaining of varying magnitudes, we can be sure that when and where the power balance shifts, employers who gain the upper hand will drive out the unions. It is not, as the Bluestones say, because "tempers have flared on both sides of the fence" that times are hard for the labor movement. Its decline is the entirely predictable result of economic and political conditions prevailing in this country over the past twenty years.

No one who believes in labor's cause would want to deny the ideals of industrial democracy espoused by the Bluestones. They may even be right to claim that American competitiveness would be well served by an Enterprise Compact. The nub of their problem is not so much about ends but over means—of how we go from here to there. Their reading of recent history, instructive as it is, has misled them. The labor-management settlement after World War II represented not a norm but very much an exception in trade-union history. What gave legitimacy to the management-rights clause was the belief that the General Electrics and U.S. Steels of this world were masters of their economic fates. The unions could take the money and leave the decisions to management. But that choice has not always been open to unions, and where the interests of their members demanded it they have in fact driven deeply into what we would today define as the realm of management. Anyone who wants to understand the history of coal mining in America, for example, would do better studying John L. Lewis than the career of any mine operator, or, for the garment trades, the lives of Sidney Hillman and David Dubinsky. And where the cutthroat conditions that afflicted coal in Lewis's time begin to be approximated in today's industries, we see a similar kind of strategic union thinking emerging.

For its part, concession bargaining also leads in interesting directions, as, for example, the company stakes being taken by airline unions; or the extensive management role by the steel union in the formerly bankrupt LTV and Wheeling-Pittsburgh firms; or, in the latest negotiating round, the seats the union has won on the boards of directors of Bethlehem, National, and Inland Steel as well as a lien on specified company properties as a guarantee for pension obligations. In all these cases the starting point was a strong union; the venue was the give-and-take of collective bargaining.

Perhaps we might coin a maxim: First, power; then, maybe, cooperation. *Negotiating the Future* may have misplaced the order of things, but that doesn't mean it evoked the wrong vision or will not have contributed to the realization of that vision. Time will tell.

This review originally appeared as "The High Price of Getting Along" in *Tikkun: A Bimonthly Jewish Critique of Politics, Culture, and Society* 18 (Nov.–Dec. 1993): 91–94. Reprinted with permission.

Thomas A. Kochan, Harry B. Katz, and Robert B. McKersie, *The Transformation of American Industrial Relations* (1986, reprint, 1994)

When this book appeared in 1986 it was widely hailed as the industrial-relations book of its generation. It arrived on the scene at a peculiarly opportune moment. Union density had plummeted, collective bargaining was everywhere in retreat, and corporate industry was under siege and in the process of dramatic restructuring. The book offered—as its title announced—a systemic explanation for what was going on in American industrial relations. A more innovative nonunion system had overtaken the collective-bargaining system in place since the New Deal era. This argument, moreover, came armed with a full panoply of social-science tools, including a theoretical framework elaborating on John T. Dunlop's *Industrial Relations Systems* (1958), a model of institutional change, substantial quantitative analysis, and an impressive empirical base, much of it drawn from the authors' own investigations. As for Kochan, Katz, and McKersie, they are, of course, preeminent scholars and represent the best the industrial-relations field has to offer.

This reissue contains the 1986 text intact, with a brief reassessment by the authors, and so provides the occasion for a second look, testing the thesis, so to speak, in the light of experience. From the beginning it was apparent that the grand argument of the book was soft at its center. The authors argued that the nonunion sector had gained its edge over the union sector by utilizing the sophisticated human resource management techniques that had emerged in the 1960s. What nonunion firms actually offered their employees turns out to be no more than the benefits of unionism without the unions—equivalent wages and fringes, grievance systems, and seniority. The trick was to link these benefits to the employees' individual relationship to the company and then persuade employees that job satisfaction and personal fulfillment were achievable through that relationship, which, of course, was where human resource management came in. So it was surprising how little the book had to say specifically about this activity, and, when it came down to cases, how dim the actual assessment. No link between job satisfaction and performance had ever been proved, the authors acknowledged. And there was "little empirical support to demonstrate that improving individual attitudes and/or motivation produces lasting economic benefits to organizations." No wonder that although surveys showed quite widespread utilization of quality of work life (QWL) programs, we are told that these programs tended to be thinly rooted and short term, which is why, the authors suggested, the actual record had not been better. And then we come to the bottom line: Progressive nonunion industrial relations depend on employee trust and commitment to the firm.

Even in 1986 the authors could not fail to recognize the fragility of that rock-bottom requirement, given the competitive pressures and downsizing already sweeping through the economy. They in fact posited a future bifurcation, with smaller and less sheltered firms opting for a cost-cutting strategy but with exemplary firms like IBM and TRW holding to the high road of trust-based progressive labor relations. Any such expectation has, of course, been shot all to hell. So what the authors have to say today makes interesting reading. "Now more than ever," they lament, "the U.S. labor market is a place where anything and everything goes." In their theory, the crucial dynamic had been the intervention in labor policy by top management; innovative human resource management was the product of "strategic choice." "Today, very few chief executives identify themselves with the issues that are of central concern in this book"—an admission fatal to its entire thrust. The authors note instead "the ease with which management can pursue a very different [low-wage] strategy. American management has few incentives for pursuing the participatory mode of work restructuring." So they place their bets elsewhere—first, with the labor movement, whose efforts to surmount the New Deal adversarial system they had actually devoted much attention to in the 1986 text; and, second, with the federal government, in particular with the Dunlop Commission on the Future of Worker-Management Relations (of which Kochan is a member) and its consideration of shop committees. Suffice it to say that by raising these possibilities, the authors are, in effect, closing the coffin on their original hypothesis. They actually have much to contribute about why the labor movement has lost its economic grip, but the one thing they cannot say is that this had anything to do with the behavioral science wizardry of human resource management. In believing that it did, the authors are in a venerable tradition of American seekers for an industrial-relations alchemy. At least they did not pay good money for the nostrums peddled by Elton Mayo and all his successors.

This review was originally published in *Contemporary Sociology* 24 (March 1995): 254–55. Reprinted with permission of the American Sociological Association.

Sanford M. Jacoby, Modern Manors: Welfare Capitalism since the New Deal (1997)

Sanford Jacoby's book is a marvelous example of how unfolding events can undermine the fixed points of historical interpretation. Among the most secure of those fixed points in American labor history has been the notion that American welfare capitalism came to an end in the throes of the Great Depression. Historians have argued over the reasons but not about the fact that corporate welfarism gave way to the welfare state and collective bargaining during the New Deal era. After the 1970s, as trade unionism weakened, the concept of competing industrial relations systems took hold. This provides Jacoby's intellectual scaffolding, but he brings to it a historical sensibility that distinguishes his scholarship from the work of more present-minded industrial-relations scholars. The originality of Jacoby's book, in fact, arises from a historical claim. He argues that welfare capitalism did not expire in the 1930s but survived in a key group of nonunion firms and reemerged in modern guise as the dominant American industrial-relations system of our own time.

Two big ideas sustain this argument. First, Jacoby insists that we identify more systematically the firm-specific conditions that, with due regard for variety and contingency, made for welfare capitalism in its original form. Jacoby's exploration of those conditions goes well beyond other historians' studies and lays the groundwork for explaining why certain firms withstood the raging progressive forces of the 1930s. Second, Jacoby identifies a shift in the orientation of welfare capitalism, from its original parochial insularity to an active engagement with the political forces set in motion by the Great Depression. Successful welfare capitalists filled in the moat (to use Jacoby's conceit of welfare capitalism as industrial manorialism); sallied forth into the post–New Deal world; and, against all expectation, reconstituted American industrial relations in their own image.

The intersection of these two ideas makes for an interesting intellectual quandary. To develop the first idea, Jacoby undertakes case studies of Eastman Kodak, Sears, Roebuck, and Thompson Products (later TRW). These are empirically rich and analytically sophisticated chapters, models of how industrial-relations history should be written. As case studies, of course, their function is to reveal underlying patterns. But Jacoby has also chosen them because they, or the men leading them, are uniquely important in the story of welfare capitalism's engagement with the post–New Deal world.

In defending his company unions, for example, Thompson Products' Fred Crawford emerges as the key corporate architect of the Taft-Hartley revisions that turned the tables on organized labor. The Social Security system's most distinguishing feature—that it complements but does not supplant private welfare provision—is the handiwork of Kodak's Marion Folsom. In Jacoby's account of the New Deal state refashioned to accommodate modern welfare capitalism, Folsom and Crawford are indispensable actors and, insofar as they sprang from and acted for the firms that employed them, so are Kodak and Thompson Products. Sears, Roebuck was perhaps a less mandatory choice, although few other firms figured so largely in pioneering behavorial science–based personnel policy, which in Jacoby's account most distinguishes modern nonunion industrial relations. So one way of reading Jacoby's book is with this question in mind: To what extent is his exploration of the firm-specific conditions for welfare capitalism at odds with his interest in demonstrating what one might call its hegemonic modern character?

Kodak was the archetypal welfarist firm. It was big, enjoyed market dominance and stable demand for its products, operated in a weak union environment, and had strong reasons for developing an internal labor market and providing exceptional job security and benefits. Indeed, Kodak came through the Great Depression not only unscathed but also unchanged, so that in the postwar era it was the least innovative of Jacoby's three firms.

Sears, like Kodak, had size, market dominance, and deep pockets. But Sears's interest in scientific human relations, the focus of Jacoby's treatment, arose from problems of a retailer with far-flung operations and no decentralized management structure capable of supervising them. The attitude surveys, nondirective interviewing, and other techniques devised by University of Chicago social scientists enabled the central office to know what was happening in the field, be responsive to the concerns of employees (especially the big-ticket salesmen), and identify hot spots vulnerable to unionization. Indeed, management often had far keener insight into the thinking of Sears employees than the unions trying to organize them. But if the power of applied behavorial science is undoubted, it remains an open question how effectively that power was deployed by companies less pressed than Sears, Roebuck after it had transformed itself from a mail-order house into a retailing giant.

As a medium-sized Cleveland auto-parts maker, Thompson Products was in many ways atypical of the welfarist survivors of the Great Depression and, in fact, was not initially identified with the movement. But Thompson Products gradually carved out a profitable niche for itself in high-end valve production so that it had comparable welfarist resources during the 1930s and, because of the firm-specific skills of its workers, strong reasons for using those resources to secure workers' loyalty. What set Thompson apart, however, was its unremitting exposure to CIO organizers, requiring hardball tactics that other welfarist firms generally eschewed (or, in Sears's case, masked by leaving the dirty work to Nathan Shefferman's outfit). If the result was a labor law more amenable to welfare capitalism, Thompson's gritty, plant-level struggle spurring its lobbying efforts came from the other side of the tracks.

Setting Thompson Products apart also was the man who ran it after 1933, Fred Crawford. The soft underbelly of welfare capitalism is the fact that it is only company policy; the industrial justice it espouses is manufactured and contingent. Crawford, however, was the genuine article. What was policy to others was to him a matter of deep conviction, and by Jacoby's account he showed an extraordinary affinity for blue-collar workers. Welfare capitalism was likewise shaped by a commanding figure at Kodak (George Eastman, the company founder) and at Sears, Roebuck (General Robert E. Wood, architect of the firm's move into retailing). But if, as Jacoby's book implies, welfare capitalism requires leadership of this caliber, few companies would have made the grade, and still fewer today, when chief executives are not commonly the permanent fixtures that Jacoby's heroes were in their time. And, more broadly, he would be hard-pressed to replicate across the corporate spectrum the particularities he found in his three case studies.

Jacoby concludes with a meditation on the future of welfare capitalism. He comes down in the middle, acknowledging the impact of market-driven forces in our economy yet insisting that the corporation remains "a central risk-bearing institution in American society." The middle ground, I would suggest, is where Jacoby's historical inquiry bears further exploration, for between his superb study of exemplary cases and his illuminating account of welfare capitalism's broadening influence we remain uncertain as to just how deep its impact was on the modern practice of industrial relations in this country.

This review was originally published in *Industrial and Labor Relations Review* 52 (Jan. 1999): 324–26. Reprinted with permission of the *Review*.

The American Debate over
Workplace Contractualism

The following paper was delivered at the 1995 meeting of the International Industrial Relations Association in Washington, D.C. Readers are advised to put themselves in the position of the audience and understand that my remarks are pitched to foreign experts looking at the American industrial-relations system from the outside.

My topic is the American workplace and in particular the system of shop-floor organization—the realm covered in European countries by works councils and, in the United Kingdom and Australia, traditionally by shop stewards. Workplace representation in this country is in a state of flux not only because of changes at the workplace but also because, for the first time since our basic labor law—the National Labor Relations Act—was adopted in 1935, workplace representation has again become an issue of public debate.

The paradigmatic form of American workplace representation ever since the 1930s is what I have elsewhere called "workplace contractualism."[1] This refers, first of all, to an array of contractual rights at the workplace—work rules, so called—the most characteristic of which are (1) seniority as the principle governing the distribution of job opportunities; (2) pay equity lodged in a highly articulated job classification structure; and (3) just cause in matters of discipline and discharge.

To enforce these contractual rights there is a formal, well-defined grievance system, with arbitration as the final step. Equally well defined is the representational structure—shop stewards authorized to represent the employees in their departments in the grievance process. All of this must be more or less familiar to you as a peculiarly American phenomenon, with its obsession with rights and procedures. Two embedded features, however, need to be kept firmly in mind. First, workplace representation is strictly a trade-union function, not only because the union negotiates the terms governing it but also because shop stewards are agents of the union. That workplace representation might be outside its realm is a notion entirely abhorrent to the American labor movement. Second, and related to that first point, the state plays no role in setting the terms of workplace representation. All its features—not only the work rules themselves but also the grievance procedure and the representation-al structure—are determined and always alterable through collective bargaining by labor and management.

This may seem anomalous to you in light of the highly developed—perhaps even overripe—state of American labor law. The crucial thing to see is that our labor law was designed to protect the rights of employ-ees to organize and bargain collectively. The workplace fell on the other side of the line. It would be the creature of collective bargaining, not of public determination (although the courts have not been shy about in-terpreting and enforcing the privately created representation system). Although this outcome seems entirely straightforward, it has, in fact, a complex and significant history that we are just now rediscovering.

For many years workplace contractualism was celebrated as one of the triumphs of American industrial relations. The Supreme Court called it "a system of industrial self-government," "a new common law—the common law of the particular industry or particular shop." That, of course, is no longer the prevailing view. Workplace contactu-alism is today widely discredited. It is generally characterized as an "adversarial" system, compared unfavorably to the Japanese and Ger-man cooperative systems, and charged with being a major obstacle to American global competitiveness. Let me bypass considering the mer-its of these claims and simply accept them as givens in the current debate—that workplace contractualism has become dysfunctional and must be replaced by a more flexible, cooperative system of workplace relations.

One might ask, Since the adversarial system is the result of private agreement, why don't the parties scrap it and negotiate something else? In fact, of course, this is happening at Saturn, Xerox, AT&T, and other companies where cooperative agreements have been negotiated. But, in truth, it is not easy to walk away from the established system. The work-place rights of workers are hard-won, they are contractual, strong vested interests are attached to them, and many union people are not so sure that the protections they provide have become outmoded. Ironically, as the adversarial system has come under attack many labor activists who once denounced it as a bureaucratic form denying workers shop-floor autonomy are now its most vociferous defenders. It would, obviously, be much easier if we could start with a clean slate. In the meantime, the adversarial system—note that I have slipped into the usage that current-ly defines the unionized workplace—has given a strong debating advan-tage to antiunion employers. Collective bargaining, they say, is incom-patible with the cooperative relations they want with their employees.

Which leads me to the other side of the current crisis of workplace relations in this country. The onslaught against organized labor has taken a terrific toll. Where once a third of all American workers were organized, roughly a sixth are today. In the private sector probably not more than one in ten is covered by a collective-bargaining agreement. For many years there was nothing problematic, from management's standpoint, in having a labor force that lacked any mechanism for workplace representation. The smarter companies, in fact, borrowed what they wanted— seniority, grievance procedures, and fringe benefits—from the union sector. But in the past decade or so the same reform impulses that have discredited the adversarial system—I am speaking, of course, of Employee Involvement—have created a felt managerial need for shop-floor organization in the form of quality circles, safety committees, and, increasingly, shop committees dealing with a variety of issues, including the terms and conditions of employment. Under the cooperative approach, to quote the vice president in charge of human resources at Kodak, "Teams of employees become much more involved in workplace decision making, developing recommendations to improve the workplace and taking charge of their work lives." This is a characteristic management statement and behind it stands a question of undoubted force: If workers are not being represented by unions, shouldn't they have the option of some other kind of voice at the workplace?

It turns out that, under American labor law, any such alternative is illegal. In December 1992 a landmark NLRB decision, since affirmed by the Seventh Court of Appeals, found that Electromation, a nonunion firm, had violated the law by setting up shop committees. The *Electromation* decision, although entirely predictable to anyone who knew the law, caused a great furor. What sense did it make to prohibit committees, as the Kodak vice president said, that gave workers the chance for "taking charge of their work lives"? *Electromation* has set in motion a debate with far-reaching implications for the future of workplace relations in this country.

As a historian, my views normally carry no special public weight. But on this particular issue—apparently so anomalous, even mystifying— history has a peculiar resonance. The only way to understand the *Electromation* decision, and what is at stake in reversing it, is to retrace the steps that led to the underlying labor law during the early New Deal. Given the ferocious antiunionism of American employers historically (now, of course, much revived), any law encouraging collective bargaining, as this New Deal measure did, had to be centrally concerned with protecting workers from employer coercion. Defining "unfair labor practices" in the law depended at least in part on the forms of employer co-

ercion in use at the time. And because a favored strategy among the more
sophisticated was to create employee organizations they could control,
a countervailing unfair labor practice, unique at the time to American
labor law, was company domination of a labor organization.

"Company union" is the term we mostly use, but the term is mis-
leading. It did not mean what Europeans call "yellow unions" or, in Ja-
pan, enterprise unions—organizations that look like unions but are controlled or strongly influenced by employers. No, company union in this
country meant a different form of organization, a *workplace* system of
representation in which departmental delegates were elected to sit on
works councils. The result in the drafting of the Wagner Act was that
company domination of a labor organization, in the form it finally took
in Section 8a(2), was defined to include the use of facilities and kinds of
employer assistance without which no shop committee could function.
The act, in effect, made illegal any form of workplace organization concerned with the terms and conditions of employment that was not the
product of a collective-bargaining agreement. This was deliberate, arising out of the conviction that anything less was incompatible with the
right of workers to freedom of association. For this, employers, with their
unrelenting antiunionism, had only themselves to blame.

Nothing is more interesting to the historian than seeing how the past
can be expunged. The labor law, once it began operating, had the remarkable effect of wiping out its own history. Only now, when Section 8a(2)
has suddenly become a live issue, are we forced reclaim that history because, without it, we have no bearings for assessing the proposals for
change currently under consideration.

Where do we stand at the moment? One of the first actions of the
incoming Clinton administration was, in response to the *Electromation*
decision, to set up a commission chaired by John T. Dunlop to look into
the question of Section 8a(2). The Dunlop Commission served usefully
as an exploratory exercise, but the politics surrounding it—the jockeying of labor and management for advantage over labor law reform more
generally—precluded any decisive outcome. The commission recom-
mended in its final report in January 1995 that committees be permitted
to deal with the terms and conditions of employment if this activity was
incidental to their primary concern with Employee Involvement.

By then, however, the Republicans had swept into power in Congress, and they had their own ideas about Section 8a(2). Their bill is called
the Teamwork for Employees and Management Act—the TEAM Act for
short—and from its title you can see its official justification: to foster
Employee Involvement and shelter it from Section 8a(2). But that's not,

in fact, how this legislation is written. What it does is to limit the coverage of Section 8a(2)—the prohibition against company domination—to labor organizations that have or aspire to collective-bargaining agreements. Everything else would be unprotected. Employers would be free to resume the employee representation plans they had been fostering until 1935. Indeed, they would be freer because now this activity would be legitimized in the law, and Employee Involvement would give it a justifying rationale that employee representation plans had always lacked. How serious employers are about building a company-dominated system of workplace representation in this country will, I think, be demonstrated by how hard they fight for the TEAM bill and, more precisely, how hard they fight against amendments tailoring limitations on Section 8a(2) to what is actually needed to shelter Employee Involvement.

Let me close by trying to satisfy your curiosity about where the labor movement stands in this struggle over Section 8a(2). Considerable debate has gone on within the AFL-CIO. Some have pointed to history, to the fact that certain of our major unions got their start in the employee representation plans. To this is added a strategic argument. The secular trend—the rate of attrition in the unionized sector—is such that, at the rate at which new workers can be organized by conventional methods, the labor movement is certain to continue losing ground. Better to let workers have other forms of workplace representation, under whatever auspices, with the possibility that they will then begin to demand trade-union representation. There is a striking parallel to a debate going on in the United Kingdom, in that case sparked by a directive from the European Union to establish mechanisms for employee consultation over redundancies and plant closings. The Trade Union Congress leadership makes the same argument some AFL-CIO officials have made: Shop structures will be an opportunity for unions that cannot make it by traditional organizing. Only the outcome of the debate is different. The TUC welcomes the construction of nonunion representation structures, whereas the AFL-CIO has come out adamantly, vociferously, against them. It just goes to show what a difference history can make.

No one knows what the outcome of the Republican legislation will be. But the terms of debate have shifted dramatically, and, on the question of workplace representation, we may be at a real turning point. So, as you can see, you have come to Washington at an interesting moment.

Postscript: This was a "turning point" that did not turn. The Republican seizure of workplace reform from the Dunlop Commission failed, although it was a near thing. Only a Clinton veto in 1996 prevented the adoption of the TEAM Act. In Clinton's second term, however, the movement to emasculate Section 8a(2) flagged. The advent of a Republican administration in 2001 saw no revival of efforts to legalize company-initiated, shop-floor systems of representation. Why it didn't is best explained by a shift in the industrial-relations climate. After thirty years of stagnation, productivity surged in the mid-1990s. Reassured by a remarkable resurgence of American inventiveness (most famously, in information technology), American employers now stridently embraced the free market, including when it came to labor. As for German and Japanese competitors, so recently feared and emulated for "high-performance work practices," they were to be pitied for employment rigidities that kept them from shedding workers and cutting costs. "Firm loyalty—either of workers to their firm or the firm to its workers—were values of a bygone era," remarked the economist Joseph E. Stiglitz in his penetrating account of the Roaring Nineties.[2] If, in the New Economy, an ideal firm was the virtual corporation, or at any rate the corporation most adept at contracting out and casting off workers, who needed Employee Involvement or worried about the constraints of Section 8a(2)?[3]

Notes

1. David Brody, "Workplace Contractualism: A Historical/Comparative Analysis," in *Industrial Democracy in America: The Ambiguous Legacy*, ed. Nelson Lichtenstein and Howell John Harris (New York, 1992), 176–205.

2. Joseph E. Stiglitz, *The Roaring Nineties: A New History of the World's Most Prosperous Decade* (New York, 2003), 183.

3. Such constraints, in any case, had been overblown. Section 8a(2) was effective against union-busting shop committees (which had been the case with *Electromation*) and probably also against full-fledged employee representation plans (if a complaint is filed with the NLRB). The more modest work teams and participatory arrangements typical of Employee Involvement are unlikely to run afoul of the law. Employers' complaints before the Dunlop Commission that they didn't like to operate under a "cloud" of uncertainty seem like crocodile tears. The worst that can happen is that the employers would be ordered to cease and desist.

7 *On the Representation Election*

The principle that labor organizations should be free of company domination is a signatory triumph of American labor law. In chapter 5, I locate the origins of that principle in the postwar labor crisis of 1919 and, in particular, in the enunciation of the words "representatives of their own choosing." An attentive reader might therefore be surprised by the dark undertone of my comment drawing attention to the significance of that moment. The explanation is to be found in the following essay. It should be read as a counterpart to chapter 4, my essay on Section 8a(2), which is also an effort at mobilizing the historian's craft on a public issue suddenly puzzling and contested. In this instance the issue calling for explanation from the past is the representation election.

The representation election, as everyone knows, is the hallmark of our labor law. Workers vote by secret ballot about whether or not they want union representation. If a majority votes yes, the union is certified by the National Labor Relations Board, and collective bargaining begins. It all seems very democratic, and almost beyond questioning.

Yet, as everyone also knows, the law has come under heavy fire in recent years. "We have to ask," David Sickler, the AFL-CIO West Coast regional director, began a recent speech, "why the hell unions are where they are right now? Why are they, we, in a declining mode?" His answer:

This essay originally appeared as "Labor Elections: Good for Workers?" in *Dissent* (Summer 1997): 71–77. Reprinted with permission.

"Because unions are trying to make change by following the old model established by federal law." Stickler's condemnation was unequivocal. "The law that governs organizing and collective bargaining"—the law, that is, centering on the representation election—"is a failure. . . . [It] doesn't work."[1]

In this essay I want to address the paradox that a labor law democratic on its face is also a bad law for workers, or, more precisely, the paradox of a law that gives workers basic rights of association and then, through the processes of "free choice" by which they select representatives, takes away those rights. Sickler knows this to be the case—hence his fury at the law. What only history can tell him is how that law, intended by its authors to liberate workers, has ended up oppressing them.

The place to begin is with the original law, the Wagner Act of 1935. The core statement of worker rights—Section 7—needs to be quoted in full: "Employees shall have the right to self-organization, to form, join, or assist labor organizations, to bargain collectively through representatives of their own choosing, and to engage in concerted activities, for the purpose of collective bargaining or other mutual aid or protection."

In its time, this capacious language was as powerful, as compelling nationally, as civil rights would be thirty years later. And, like the great Civil Rights Act of 1964, Section 7 was a long time coming, emerging from a century-old doctrinal struggle that pitted the collective rights of workers against the rights of property and individual contract. For many years the battle had gone against labor, but gradually, and then inexorably, the balance shifted. We can trace back at least to the commission President Cleveland appointed to investigate the Pullman strike of 1894 the view that the right of workers to organize and bargain collectively ought not to be denied. We can then follow that idea into the briefly enforced wartime policy of 1917–18; the Railway Labor Act of 1926; and, by virtual acclamation during the Hoover administration, into the Norris-LaGuardia Anti-Injunction Act of 1932.

Norris-LaGuardia, in fact, already contained the gist of Section 7. All that the Wagner Act added was enforcement provisions—the unfair labor practices of Section 8 prohibiting employers from coercing employees in the exercise of their rights, dominating or assisting labor organizations, discriminating against employees for union activity, or refusing to bargain collectively with representatives of employees. There was debate over the substance of these unfair labor practices but never any question that a law seeking to enforce labor's rights would contain such provisions. A state-mandated bargaining structure—what became the rules of representation in Section 9—was something else. This had never figured in the long-evolving struggle for labor's rights but sprang from an anomalous, and probably unrepeatable, historical moment when the United States had its one serious fling with a corporatist economy.

My reference is, of course, to the National Industrial Recovery Act of 1933, which took shape during the Hundred Days, when the New Deal was scrambling to come to grips with the Great Depression. This was the place, in a massive, chaotic experiment in industrial self-regulation, where the grand objectives of Norris-LaGuardia lodged and from whence came our permanent labor law.

Exhilarated workers—free at last, so they thought—rose up and organized. Strikes erupted across the country. Fearing for economic recovery, President Roosevelt set up the National Labor Board (NLB), with Robert F. Wagner, the great urban liberal senator from New York, as its chair (and by this assignment fated to be the father of American labor law). Initially, the board's mission was solely to mediate industrial disputes. It had no responsibility, nor any agenda, for implementing Section 7(a), which asserted labor's rights and was attached to every NRA code of fair competition. Nor was there even a conception of the representation structure that would be enacted in 1935. There was no model for this anywhere in the industrialized world and no substantial precedent in America's own experience, which had been, in this realm strictly off-limits to government interference.

"As to what steps are necessary to take," explained the secretary of Wagner's board, the veteran labor-relations expert William L. Leiserson, "we can only say that is a matter for the employees to decide for themselves." In the board's view, "the selection of a form of organization and the designation of representatives, as well as the method of designation, are placed by Section 7(a) within the exclusive control of the workers." Yet it was precisely the choice of forms of organization and methods of designation—"this freedom of self-organization" as the NLB called it—that the Wagner Act ultimately did take from workers and arrogate to the state.[2]

That happened because of the way open-shop employers responded to Section 7(a). They dared not oppose it in principle—any more than, say, Texaco today dares claim it did right by discriminating against black employees—but they did have a strategy. In a great rush, they set up company unions in which workers appeared to be exercising their rights but which, of course, the company controlled. These creations were not fake trade unions but a different animal altogether. They were works councils or, in the more common usage, employee representation plans and hence *systemically* different from trade unions. Once Senator Wagner concluded that the company unions violated Section 7(a)—"the employer has no right to initiate a plan of organization, or to participate in any way, in the absence of any request from the employees, in their designation of representatives and their self-organization"—he had to meet them on their own terrain; that is, he had to advance a representation system that *was* compatible with Section 7(a).[3] This happened piecemeal, case by case as disputes came before Wagner's board, but the drift was unmistakably toward state-mandated representation—ultimately, a privileged bargaining structure that granted the right of exclusive representation to unions demonstrating support by a majority of workers and requiring the employer to bargain with unions so certified, and them alone, for those workers.[4]

The irony is that the reason for this NLRB-administered system evaporated once the law was enacted because the company unionism that had called it forth simultaneously became illegal. Section 82—8a(2) under Taft-Hartley—defined company domination of labor organizations so stringently that workplace representation in any form not stemming from collective bargaining was—and still is—effectively proscribed. Too late. The die was cast. The associational rights of workers—"this freedom of self-organization"—had fused with a specific state-mandated process for determining and certifying bargaining agents.

And now, at their moment of triumph, the authors of the Wagner Act faced a dilemma of their own making. They had created, in this representation system, a platform for the coercion of workers by employers. The problem, keenly understood by these veterans of the battle against company unionism, was coercive speech. What an employer says, noted the Twentieth Century Fund spokesman in testifying for the law, "so easily leads to what is coercion and fear." All it takes is to "go to a man whose bread and butter is dependent on your pay envelop and suggest to him you think it would be a good thing for him to form a company union."[5]

That was why, during the NRA period, Wagner's labor board had fashioned a common law of employer neutrality. Before a representation election employers could not say that workers would be better off voting one way or another, that the plant would close if the outside union won, that concessions would be forthcoming if the company union won, or that individuals would be rewarded or punished for how they voted. In short, as a Brookings Institution study summed it up, "The election was nothing with which the employer need be concerned. It was a matter in which his employees alone had a stake."[6]

This claim—that when workers chose bargaining agents under NLRB supervision they were really engaging in self-organization—justified employer neutrality. Wagner, as best he could, sustained that claim in his law. Thus, for example, his "one-sided" treatment of employers, who alone were subject to unfair labor-practice prohibitions, or, equally telling, how Wagner handled what we have taken to be the capstone provision, the representation election. Despite a lot of rhetoric, Wagner actually minimized the election. It was "nothing but an investigation, a factual determination of who are the representatives of employees."[7] An election, in fact, was not mandatory in the Wagner Act; at the discretion of the NLRB, "any other suitable method" would do.

Self-organization and employer neutrality went together. "The employer has no place in elections," insisted Francis Biddle, Wagner's successor at the NRA, because the election is "a mere inquiry into the facts."[8] To employer complaints that the law was one-sided, Wagner responded that workers did not presume to interfere when their employers organized (and had been doing so with great abandon under the aegis of the NRA), so why should employers interfere when workers organized? They "must leave the worker alone during an election."[9]

In the early Wagner Act years, the NLRB treated antiunion statements unequivocally as unfair labor practices. "In the final analysis, most of this propaganda, even when it contains no direct or even indirect threat, is aimed at the worker's fear of loss of his job." Next to actual or threatened dismissals, the NLRB considered such speech "the most common form of interference with self-organization." Employers got the message. If you want to avoid trouble, a 1940 legal manual for employers advised, "Stay *completely neutral* regarding elections."[10] The underpinning in self-organization doctrine likewise was robust. The NLRB regularly certified unions by means of card checks, the inspection of membership lists, and even the NLRB examiner's impression of majority support at a factory meeting. Nearly a third of all certifications in 1938 and 1939 occurred without an election.

But at its core, NLRB certification was not self-organization. Employers hammered away at the claim that it was, but the decisive blow was cast, remarkably, not by employers but by Wagner's own NLRB. The law had not anticipated that organized labor would split apart over industrial unionism or that representation campaigns would become an AFL-CIO battleground in which employers might sometimes be caught in a standoff between rival unions. In this situation, the NLRB ruled in *Cudahy* (1939), the employer could require an election, even if documentary evidence hitherto considered adequate showed that one of the unions had a majority. A week later in another meatpacking case (*Armour and Co.*) the board broadened the rule to apply to cases where there was no rival union. At the behest of the employer the election became mandatory for certification of a union as bargaining agent.

Why had the NLRB done this? In part, for political reasons. It was besieged at the time by charges, not wholly unfounded, that it was communist-infested and pro-CIO and besieged also by an unholy alliance of the AFL and organized industry threatening legislation to rein in the board. *Cudahy* was a bone thrown to the board's tormentors. But that was the least of it. The board had gotten caught up in its own bureaucratic processes (the official explanation was that *Cudahy*, by reducing "doubt and disagreement" about employee preferences, would make for better bargaining relations after certification) and had lost sight of why the mechanisms for choosing representatives had been left open.[11]

We can best track this diminishing sensibility at the point of where administrative process and self-organization clashed most directly. This was over bargaining unit determination, which was, of course, inherent in any representation scheme and bound to be delegated to the agency administering the scheme. But bargaining unit trenched on union jurisdiction, and jurisdiction was a hallmark of self-organization. Acknowledging its trespass, the NLRB at first deferred to the AFL, keeping hands off even in the face of jurisdictional disputes between affiliated unions. As for making unit determinations, the NLRB held that the factors it weighed primarily derived from self-organization. Insofar as possible, it "utilized the experienced judgment of the workers themselves as to the existence of the mutual interest in working conditions which must exist among members of an appropriate unit." This faith in "the experienced judgment of the workers themselves" eventually translated, under the Globe Doctrine (1938), into the procedural right of craft workers to indicate by secret ballot whether they wanted separate bargaining units. The trigger, as with *Cudahy*, was the AFL-CIO rivalry, and, as with *Cudahy*, the Globe Doctrine marked the ascendancy of administrative process. Soon enough the language of self-organization that had suffused unit determination was gone.[12] Although hugely important to battling unions at the time (and later in the arsenal of antiunion employers), unit determination was a secondary feature of the representation scheme but one that accurately registered its drift away from self-organization.

It was but a short step from *Cudahy* to Taft-Hartley, which in 1947 made the election mandatory for certification. A union might still gain exclusive bargaining rights without an election and without benefit of NLRB certification, but it was left to the employer to assess the union's claim of majority standing. Moreover, Taft-Hartley attached specific advantages to certification, including a nonchallengeable year and protection against organizational picketing.

With the election now the core process, Taft-Hartley undertook a telling repositioning of the law. Unions became subject, like employers, to unfair labor practices; employers, like unions, gained the right to petition for elections. They had become, in the eyes of the law, equal players in an electoral game. As for the workers, Section 7 now said they could refrain from as well as act on their rights of association. In the symbolism of the representation election this said that a worker was just a voter making a choice between collective and individual bargaining.

The Supreme Court had already, in 1941, taken cognizance of the free-speech rights of employers in *NLRB v. Virginia Electric and Power.* Employer speech could be regulated but not by any blanket rule of employer neutrality. By the postwar period, the NLRB had given ground and little remained of the original bar against employer speech. Then Taft-Hartley inserted a free-speech provision into the law: "The expressing of any view, argument, or opinion, or the dissemination thereof, whether in written, printed, graphic, or visual form, shall not constitute or be evidence of an unfair labor practice under any provision of this Act, if such expression contains no threat of reprisal or force or promise of benefit" (Section 8[c]).

It had been the premise of the Wagner Act that the only way to assure employee free choice was to bar employers from the process. Now, with Taft-Hartley, the time came for testing that premise. Was there, in effect, a middle ground on which employer free speech and employee free choice might coexist? The courts and the NLRB have sought this ground in two ways, first, by trying to define, through a variety of tests, what constitutes impermissible employer speech, and, second, by a balancing of the conflicting rights of employers to speak and of workers to associate freely.[13]

Immediately, however, a second employer right—the right of property—entered the equation. In its simplest form, this involved the question of solicitation. Should unions have the same access that employers did to workers on company property? No, the Supreme Court ruled in *NLRB v. Babcock and Wilcox* (1956), except where workers are so physically isolated—say, in a lumber camp or cannery—that they are beyond the reach of the union. *Lechmere v. NLRB* (1992) reaffirmed that standard.

And what about that other property right of the employer, ownership in the labor of his employees? Because the employer has bought their time, can he make them listen? The NLRB had always regarded "captive audience" meetings as coercive and barred them. In 1948 the board declared captive audience meetings lawful but went on in *Bonwit Teller v. NLRB* (1951) to assert the correlative right of unions to reply. In 1953 the Eisenhower board in *Livingston Shirt* rejected this equal-access claim, and the Supreme Court agreed, provided that organizers had other access to employees. As things presently stand, access to employees at the workplace is exclusively (save in isolated settings) the prerogative of the employer.

Interrogating workers, like captive audience speeches, was originally prohibited as inherently coercive. Then, in *Blue Flash* (1954), the NLRB said no, interrogation could not itself be proscribed, only those interrogations in which coercion could be demonstrated. A jungle of case law has grown up around *Blue Flash*, but no amount of fine distinctions about time, place, and so on can alter the fact that, in the heat of a representation campaign, an interview in the supervisor's office about how an employee feels about the company is coercive to that employee.

The same unreality pervades the case law on Taft-Hartley limits on free speech. Threats and promises are prohibited, but what constitutes a "threat" or a "promise?" That it is more than a prediction, the Supreme Court in its wisdom decided in *Gissel v. NLRB* (1969). This distinction between threat and prediction currently defines the scope of protected employer free speech. Employers cannot say they will close the plant if the union wins, but they can say that their customers will go elsewhere or point to neighboring unionized plants that went out of business. And they can describe their bargaining tactics should the union win, with negotiations starting from scratch and no guarantee that employees will not end up worse than before, even, if they chose to strike, no jobs at all. *Gissel* is duck soup for lawyers. No employer need fear that, with the right counsel, he cannot safely make "predictions" that scare the pants off his employees.

It is not as if the courts have been blind to the power realities on the shop floor. Indeed, *Gissel* was eloquent about the dangers of equating an NLRB election with a political election, "where the independent voter may be freer to listen more objectively and employers as a class freer to talk." Nor have we lacked for standards of what constitutes a fair representation election. In *General Shoe* (1948) the Truman NLRB held up a "laboratory standard" it intended to enforce. Elections must "be conducted, under conditions as nearly ideal as possible, to determine the uninhibited desires of the employees."

For all its brave words, *General Shoe*, like *Gissel*, only demonstrated the futility of the law of employer free speech. *General Shoe*'s "laboratory standard" gave rise to another luxuriant case law, fascinating for the distinctions it developed between the permissible and impermissible in misrepresentations of fact, racist appeals, third-party actions, and so on but of no real account for purposes of preventing "an atmosphere calculated to render a free choice improbable." The remedy for infractions that disqualify an election on the basis of the laboratory standard is only another election. And below the screen of that standard the determined employer interrogates workers; requires them to attend captive-audience meetings; in multitudinous ways available to him pressures them relentlessly; and, if they remain uncowed, makes their lives miserable and their futures bleak.

I have written so far only of what is currently lawful, not of the unfair labor practices that, in this hostile atmosphere, accompany the antiunion campaign. Workers are fired every day for union activities, and nonunion workers know it. This rampant lawlessness is not different, in its sources, from the lawful assault on "free choice" that began after Taft-Hartley. Once representation was reconceived to be an electoral contest, either outcome became legitimate. If the union won, it got bargaining rights; if the company won, it got a "union-free environment." What would once have been inadmissible (employers spoke piously of the "open shop" in the old days) now became, on the fair-and-square basis of the election, respectable and brazenly espoused by the National Association of Manufacturers and its Council for a Union-Free Environment. So did the means it took to win. The gloves came off in the late 1950s. Within a decade the number of NLRB unfair labor practices tripled, and by 1980 it stood at a record thirty-five thousand. By the labor law scholar Paul Weiler's count, one worker was being illegally discharged for every twenty union votes cast.

The prohibition against discrimination for union activity is the most basic and unimpeachable in the law. Yet employers routinely violate it and accept the back pay penalty as a cost of doing business. By the time workers are reinstated, the union has long since been crushed, and few workers who are reinstated actually stay around for long. What had begun as fundamental to labor's rights has ended as an incident of the representation election, an item in play in the hardball that determines whether employers preserve their union-free environment. This lawlessness does not merely vitiate free choice. It attacks the integrity of labor's fundamental rights and drains the law of the moral content that had brought it into being in the first place.

Unions today consider it a big victory when they extract from employers a promise to be "neutral" in a representation campaign. No one seems to remember that employer neutrality was once what the law itself required. This had been Senator Wagner's doing. But so, sadly, was its undoing, because the law that Wagner wrote had built into it the conditions that eventually killed employer neutrality. Once free choice came to be synonymous with electoral choice, it followed that employers would be seen as parties to the process, that their "free speech" rights would then prevail, and that we would end up more or less as we have, with employer domination of the representation election.

David Sickler knows the representation election is bad for workers. He should also know it has no moral claim on them. The idea that it is somehow inherent or inevitable in a law protecting the associational rights of workers is wrong. History says otherwise. State-administered representation had no original place in the law's Section 7 rights but emerged without design from the miasma of this country's one fling with corporatism. Its core process, the mandatory election, came as a still later accretion on the law and has evolved, in ways I have described, into a formidable constraint on the exercise of rights that the law still says American workers have.

Knowing this history, we can think more productively about how to write a better law or, until then, how to make the best of the present one. And we could mind the admonition of the chief drafter of the Wagner Act, Leon Keyserling, about not forgetting "where Labor's strength really lies" and believing that unions might be built up "with[out] anything to hold them together but some rule of law based upon distorted political analogies."[14] This was in a private letter. Too bad he didn't say it in public.

Notes

1. *Labor Research Review*, no. 24 (1996): 101–9.

2. Christopher L. Tomlins, *The State and the Unions: Labor Relations, Law, and the Organized Labor Movement in America* (New York, 1985), 113.

3. National Labor Board, *Decisions* (Washington, D.C., 1934), 19.

4. The evolution of these principles can be followed in the compiled NLB *Decisions*; in an authoritative contemporary study, Lewis L. Lorwin and Arthur Wubnig, *Labor Relations Boards* (Washington, D.C., 1935); and in a thoroughly researched modern account, James A. Gross, *The Making of the National Labor Relations Board: A Study in Economics, Politics, and the Law* (Albany, 1974).

5. National Labor Relations Board, *Legislative History of the National Labor Relations Act, 1935*, 2 vols. (Washington, D.C., 1959, repr. 1985), 2:2100.

6. Lorwin and Wubnig, *Labor Relations Boards*, 160–61.

7. *Legislative History*, 1:1426, 2:2314.

8. Ibid., 1:1473–74.

9. Ibid., 1:1236.

10. National Labor Relations Board, *First Annual Report* (Washington, D.C.,

1936), 73–74; W. A. Rickhoff and Harvey B. Rector, *Procedures and Practices under the National Labor Relations Board* (Cincinnati, 1940), 14.

11. NLRB, *Fifth Annual Report* (Washington, D.C., 1940), 60–61.

12. Compare the discussion of unit determination in NLRB, *Third Annual Report* (Washington, D.C., 1938), 156ff. and *Fifth Annual Report*, 82 ff. Quotations from the *Third Annual Report*, 160; and Gross, *The Making of the NLRB*, 245.

13. The summary account that follows scarcely captures the contested legal history of the modern labor law. Readers interested in the politics behind that history, and the doctrinal marches and countermarches, are urged to consult the excellent final installment of James A. Gross's NLRB trilogy, *Broken Promises: The Subversion of U.S. Labor Relations Policy, 1947–1994* (Philadelphia, 1995).

14. Leon Keyserling to A. L. Wirin, Dec. 9, 1936 (copy), folder 51, Robert L. Wagner Papers, Georgetown University Library.

8 *Freedom and Solidarity in American Labor Law*

Just as I was finishing the preceding account of the NLRB election, an invitation arrived to join a labor-oriented project sponsored by the Center for the Study of Freedom at Washington University in St. Louis. The assigned topics were wide-ranging, with papers on slavery in the early modern world and in Britain and the Caribbean and serfdom in Russia. There were also various American themes, including mine on trade unionism. I assumed that what was wanted was a paper that ranged back to origins, which this essay does. It had seemed initially an undertaking unrelated to the other chapters in this volume until, as I proceeded, I found otherwise. The symbiotic relationship I posited between the contemporary and the historical is nowhere more plainly revealed than in what follows.

It would be a contradiction in terms to speak of a trade union of slaves or serfs. Indeed, the rise of trade unionism is entwined in the great arc of labor's liberation that is the common history of all the Western industrializing countries. Yet the condition of freedom, essential though it be, stands

This essay originally appeared as "Free Labor, Law, and American Trade Unionism," in *The Terms of Labor: Slavery, Serfdom, and Free Labor*, edited by Stanley Engerman © 1999 by the Board of Trustees of the Leland Stanford Jr. University. By permission of the publisher.

in an uneasy relationship to trade unionism. The problem, as the English jurist A. V. Dicey framed it a century ago, is that individual liberty encompasses "the right of combined action," but this right threatens individual liberty. The dilemma "is at bottom always and everywhere the same" but not its resolution, because, in principle, there is no way to bring "into harmony two essentially conflicting rights, namely the right to individual freedom and the right of association." The most that can be achieved is a "rough compromise," which manifestly each country must find for itself.[1] In this essay I want to explore how, in the domain of employment, the United States grappled with Dicey's "theoretically insoluble problem" and, more particularly, why the rough compromise it arrived at so burdened the reception of trade unionism in American labor law.

The Invention of Free Labor

In the beginning, of course, the notion of free labor was itself a contradiction in terms. In early English law, work was compulsory for every able-bodied person without visible means of support, and the terms of employment—wages, work time, and length of service—were matters of state policy. Although not required to do so, the Colonies, having no other model to draw on, treated the Tudor industrial code as their starting point for labor regulation but without the administrative superstructure available in the home country. The colonial governments never, for example, duplicated the royal oversight of wage-fixing by the English justices of the peace. The history of colonial labor regulation is thus clouded, embedded in the court records of townships, parishes, and counties. Thanks to the indefatigable scholarship of Richard B. Morris many years ago, however, we have a good idea of how closely colonial practice conformed to and then, very quickly, diverged from the Tudor industrial code.[2] Colonial conditions had a liberating effect, but so did an ideological shift experienced on both sides of the Atlantic.

The medieval idea of labor as a resource at the community's command gave way to what C. B. MacPherson has called "possessive individualism"—the conviction arising out of the seventeenth-century English revolution that man is born free and that "freedom is proprietorship of one's own person and capacities."[3] For labor, the implications of possessive individualism were ambiguous. There was, remarks Robert J. Steinfeld, "a deep tension between the idea that the social order was composed of naturally equal, essentially uniform, autonomous individuals and the notion that the labor agreement, which involved the selling of one's most basic property, the property in one's own energies, left some individuals under the control of other individuals, in a sense as their property."[4] The resolution of that tension came by finding a way of making work entered into voluntarily, by contract, definitively, and absolutely "free," hence the title of Steinfeld's book on which I am relying, *The Invention of Free Labor.*

The tool of invention, Steinfeld argues, was the provision in the Tudor industrial code compelling workers to perform agreed-upon services on pain of imprisonment. This principle was routinely enforced by colonial courts in the early years but seems by the early eighteenth century to have lapsed for laborers and artisans and within another half-century for hired servants as well.[5] In England, by contrast, the coercive enforcement of labor agreements remained robust. In 1823 a new master and servant law reaffirmed criminal sanctions for breach of labor contracts, and until far into the nineteenth century English workers were routinely prosecuted and imprisoned under that provision of the law.[6]

On the Continent, restrictions on mobility tended to be enforced administratively. Belgian and French workers were by law required to carry a *livret*, or work passport, showing that they had fulfilled their obligations to previous employers. Swedish workers were prohibited from changing jobs except at an annual break period, and anyone without work could be prosecuted for being "unprotected" and assigned to compulsory service.[7] In central and eastern Europe, the heavy hand of the police reinforced the constraints on labor mobility. "An atmosphere of permanent suspicion and surveillance" pervaded mid-century Germany, writes Jürgen Kocka, burdening traveling journeymen "under the elaborate system of passports, obligatory travel records, work licenses, and prohibitions" and for practical purposes making any movement dependent on the assent of their employers.[8] In Prussia, as part of the liberalizing economic reforms of 1845, industrial employment became contractual, but with penal sanctions against workers who violated their agreements.

If the range of freedom was greater in America, so, paradoxically, was the range of servitude. Not from any sense of superiority over Europe but from contradictions within their own country did Americans arrive at a final definition of free labor. The biggest contradiction arose from the curse of slavery. In itself, however, slavery was not problematic because, as an involuntary condition, it was clearly distinct from free labor and doubly distinct because it was associated with race. But slavery was not America's only system of bondage. Roughly half the immigrants arriving from Europe before the 1820s came as indentured servants, bound to service under terms markedly harsher than those generally countenanced by the Tudor code. For practical purposes, indentured servants were the property of the owner of their indentures. They could be moved, sold, or rented, and if they ran off, they were subject to pursuit and forceable return. Yet indentured servitude fell within the bounds of possessive individualism because it was conceived to be a contractual arrangement freely arrived at between consenting individuals.

Indentured servitude demonstrated that, into the years of the early Republic, Americans had not yet divested themselves of the received assumption that, in Steinfeld's words, "legal freedom (and unfreedom) were not absolute matters but matters of degree." This meant not, as in earlier times, that all labor was in some degree unfree but rather that, between freedom and unfreedom, there might exist a third state. Indentured servants occupied, as a court said in 1793, "a middle rank between slaves and freemen."⁹ The bias of indentured servitude, however, was toward freedom—voluntary servitude, not partial slavery.

That bias, ironically, was thrown into doubt by slave emancipation in the northern states after the American Revolution. Under these emancipating laws, indentured servitude was used to hold in bondage the first beneficiaries—children born after the state laws went into effect—until full maturity, generally age twenty-eight. Still more compromising were the uses slaveholders found for indentured servitude when they moved to free states. Their lawyers held that indentures entered into by slaves were good contracts because of the consideration received in being delivered from slavery. Steinfeld cites a series of Pennsylvania decisions accepting this appalling line of reasoning.¹⁰ The effect, however, was to challenge the very rationale on which indentured servitude depended, namely, that it was *voluntary*.

The Northwest Ordinance of 1785 already offered a solution in the concept of involuntary servitude, which, along with slavery, was proscribed in the states created under the Ordinance's mandate. In *The Case of Mary Clark, a Woman of Color* (1821), the Supreme Court of Indiana tested indentured servitude against that constitutional provision. Mary Clark had, as an adult and a free black, consented to serve for twenty years. Was the contract she had signed binding on her? No, the court ruled, because she would then be "in a state of involuntary servitude." The condition of free labor required, no matter what the terms of agreement, that employment be "at the will of the employee."¹¹

This, says Steinfeld, was the moment of invention, conjuring out of the crisis over indentured servitude the American doctrine of free labor. The employment practice that rubbed against the right of departure—the time contract—began to disappear after mid-century. It was supplanted by employment at will, the contractual apotheosis of free labor. If the worker's right to leave was absolute, so was the employer's to dismiss him or her.

In Europe, specific performance began to be abandoned half a century after *Mary Clark*. Only in 1875, after a robust campaign by the emerging labor movement, did England repeal criminal sanctions for breach of employment contracts. Prussia had done the same for industrial workers six years earlier. France ended the law requiring work passports in 1890. Across Europe and in Canada and Australia the laws enforcing labor contracts were gone by the early twentieth century.

In light of this history, the rejection of enforceable agreements by American courts might be seen merely as the opening chapter in an international movement against contractual constraints on workers. But within that common history the differences of meaning bear emphasis. Much more than in America, where practice long preceded court doctrine, European workers gained an actual expansion of personal freedom from the abolition of coercive performance. Yet that particular advance had comparatively little ideological resonance in Europe or, at least, not a resonance picked up by the historians of European labor. And this in turn suggests, as a third point of difference, the potency of law in the processes of ideological formation in America. The right to depart, Steinfeld's work implies, served in this way: It was the core legality underpinning a conception of free labor that imagined American labor relations as a universe of independent and equal individuals. Very much in America's encounter with trade unionism turned on this ideo-legal formulation.

We can better appreciate the relationship between law and ideology by attending to a speech delivered by Henry Williams, a Taunton lawyer, in the debate over the secret ballot at the Massachusetts constitutional convention of 1853:

> In a free government like ours employment is simply a contract between parties having equal rights. The operative agrees to perform a certain amount of work in consideration of receiving a certain amount of money. The work to be performed is, by the contract, an equivalent for the money paid. The relationship, when properly entered into, is therefore one of mutual benefit. The employed is under no greater obligation to the employer than the employer is to the employed. . . . In the eye of the law, they are both freemen—citizens having equal rights, and brethren having one common destiny.[12]

Williams's speech is illuminating in at least three ways. First, it offers a spacious account of the law of free labor, at the core of which was the principle of equal rights—the law treats, without distinction, employers and workers alike. Their relationship is likewise governed by an equality of obligation, no more and no less than the terms of contract. The law of free labor, however, extends beyond employment and encompasses the equal rights of workers as "freemen" and "citizens," a precocious achievement in the form of suffrage (for white males) of the early American Republic.[13] All this was in larger terms appropriate, politically, "in a free government like ours" and, socially, between classes that are "brethren having one common destiny."

Second, there is what might be called the pseudo-reality of law revealed in Williams's speech. He speaks as if he is describing a world of free and equal individuals. But Williams knows that not to be the case. On the contrary, he says, the employment relationship is cruelly unequal, exposing workers to coercion by employers and imperiling the democratic process. "The practice of intimidation has become with us an evil of great magnitude," but it is an evil not easily dealt with "because every man has a right to employ, or to dismiss from his employment, whom he pleases."[14] We have mistaken one face of the law for another. The law is real, of course, invoked every day by myriad citizens going about the business of life. But the law also describes an imagined world—in this instance, of free and equal workers—that encompasses what these same citizens valued and wanted to believe to be true. It is in this particular sense that law can be called ideological and, more specifically, that the law of employment translates into the ideology of free labor.

Third, from Williams's speech we get a suggestion of the utility of law as ideology. Williams invokes it as a kind of resource, mobilized to advance the case he is making, which is, in this instance, the adoption of the secret ballot. Others might have different cases to make, but insofar as they were arguing about labor, the ideology of free labor would serve in the same way. Thus Williams's chief protagonist, Otis P. Lord of Salem, accuses him of undermining the independence vital to a system of free labor. The secret ballot "is, in its nature, calculated to, and actually does, diminish the self-respect of the voter" by assuming his cowardice and need for protection from his employer. "Any such imputation . . . is unworthy of them. They are not a craven, miscreant class of men, who are afraid to look upon the face of day to vote."[15]

For purposes of this essay, the question is how free-labor ideology—for which Williams's words provide the text—was mobilized in the nation's encounter with trade unionism, which was, of course, how workers themselves responded to the imbalance of power that was Williams's true subject.

The Reception of Trade Unionism

No state regime ever welcomed the onset of working-class organization. Across Europe the first response was outright repression. In France, the Chapelier Act of 1791 declared gatherings of workers "riotous" meetings whose participants would be "dispersed by force" and subject to severe punishment. The Penal Code of 1810 outlawed any "coalition on the part of the workingmen to cease work at the same time, to forbid work in a shop, to prevent the coming or leaving before or after certain hours, and in general, to suspend, hinder or make dear labor."[16] The Federal Congress of German States in 1840 unified the policies of its members against workers "who have committed offenses against the State Government through participation in illicit combinations, journeymen's societies, and boycotts" and declared strikes "rebellious disturbances against the constituted authorities." Prussia's Industrial Code of 1845 prohibited meetings of workers to obtain better conditions and required that workers' societies of any kind receive police authorization.[17] Even in Britain, where criminal conspiracies under the common law already applied, Parliament saw fit to enact draconian Combination acts from 1721 onward covering specific occupations and, in 1799 and 1800, banning trade unions altogether.

Such laws were unknown in America. Not that the early journeymen's unions were welcomed—courts condemned them as "self-created societies," gaining "unrighteous advantages by means of disciplined and confederated numbers"—nor even that their legal standing was initially any more secure.[18] But the danger posed by unions was differently defined. Where in Europe they threatened the state, unions in America threatened fellow citizens. Hence, while in Europe policy over trade unionism was an affair of state, in America it was an affair of the courts, guided not by enacted legislation or executive fiat but by the English common law, on which the courts drew as disputes by aggrieved private individuals came before them. As decision built on decision, precedent by precedent, an American law of trade unionism took shape.

In 1806 the mayor's court of Philadelphia, Moses Levy presiding, heard for the first time a case charging American workers—in this instance, the city's journeymen shoemakers—with criminal conspiracy.[19] The common law, Levy instructed the jury, "says there may be cases in which what one man may do without offence, many combined may not do with impunity."[20] In the case before him, the shoemakers had undertaken to raise the prices on their work. Any one of them might freely have done this, and so indeed might the entire group if such was "individually the opinion of all." The conspiracy was "that they were bound down by their agreement, and pledged by mutual engagements to persist in it, however contrary to their own judgment."[21] The essence of the crime, therefore, was the fact of association, the rules and obligations welding workers into a collective body. There is no other way of reading Levy's holding than as a condemnation of trade unionism per se and not different, in principle, from the repressive standard then prevailing across Europe.

Whether the English common law even applied after independence, however, was a question that bitterly divided Anglophile Federalists from Jeffersonian Republicans just as the conspiracy indictments in *Commonwealth v. Pulis* came down against the Philadelphia shoemakers in 1805. Their lawyers argued strenuously that no legal basis existed in Pennsylvania for the indictments.[22]

Moses Levy would have none of it. He directed the jury to ignore, as immaterial and improper, the defense's claim "that the spirit of the revolution and the principle of the common law are opposite in this case" or that applying it "would operate an attack upon the rights of man." The foundation of justice, pronounced Levy, was the common law far more than the legislature, whose enactments are only the "temporary emanations" of a "fluctuating political body." The common law "regulates with a sound discretion most of our concerns in civil and social life. Its rules are the result of the wisdom of the ages." Only those who knew it intimately and in its entirety—the inner sanctum of lawyers—were "competent judges of it." The courts, in their "laborious" pursuit of justice, ought never be impugned because "from that moment the security of persons and property is gone."[23]

Levy's views prevailed—an echo, of course, of the more general triumph of law in the American polity that legal historians have been exploring.[24] American labor law thus became for the next century preeminently a judicial prerogative and, unlike Britain, out of reach of Recorder Levy's "fluctuating political bod[ies]." Judge-made labor law, more than any other proximate fact, distinguishes the state regulation of unions in America from that of Britain or, indeed, any European country until far into the twentieth century.[25]

Still, Levy's indictment of trade unions clearly would not do, not in republican America, with its citizen workers and enshrined rights of assembly. Almost at once the courts began to scramble to more defensible grounds. In the next conspiracy trial, against New York shoemakers who had struck to enforce their rule against working alongside expelled members, the judge acknowledged their "right to meet and regulate their concerns, and to ask for wages, and to work or refuse," but he found "the means they used were of a nature too arbitrary and coercive, and . . . went to deprive their fellow-citizens of rights as precious as any they contend for."[26] Thus, only three years after *Commonwealth v. Pulis*, the chink was already opening through which lawful combination might slip. But what well-placed Benthamite parliamentarians in Britain initiated with dispatch in 1824 took in America the labors of the courts in several state jurisdictions over three and a half decades.[27] It also took the mounting crisis of the 1830s to bring forth, in *Commonwealth v. Hunt* (1842), the definitive opinion of the chief justice of Massachusetts, Lemuel Shaw.[28]

The essence of the charge against the Boston bootmakers in the case under appeal before him, Shaw wrote, was "that the defendants and others formed themselves into a society, and agreed not to work for any person, who should employ any journeyman or other person, not a member of such society, after notice given him to discharge such workman. The manifest intent of the association is, to induce all those engaged in the same occupation to become members of it. Such a purpose is not unlawful."[29] With these words Shaw put American unionism on the right side of the law.

But unions were not thereby shielded from conspiracy law. On the contrary, Shaw's purpose was to defend the integrity of that doctrine and fix labor activity securely under the scrutiny of the courts. The law of labor conspiracy, however, was too flawed an instrument. The precedents, as they came down to him, did not enable Shaw to frame "any definition or description . . . which shall specifically identify this offense—a description broad enough to include all cases punishable under this description, without including acts which are not punishable."[30]

The problem distinguishing Massachusetts from Britain was that Massachusetts had no equivalent for the statutory wage controls whose violation had figured in the foundational English case *Rex v. Cambridge Tailors* (1721). Shaw's remedy was technical, focusing as it did on the sufficiency of the indictment. Shaw agreed with the brilliant defense counsel Robert Rantoul that inasmuch as conspiracy was a criminal act, it required indictments as rigorous as those applying in criminal cases generally. The gist of Shaw's masterly argument—brought off, as Walter Nelles remarks, with "an old-style technical rigor"—was to demonstrate, point by point, how the indictment in the case before him fell short of that standard and warranted a reversal of the lower court and discharge of the bootmakers.[31]

Embedded in this technical argument, however, was Chief Justice

Shaw's meditation on the nature of labor conspiracy itself—"a question of great importance to the Commonwealth." On two central issues, he laid down conclusions that rightly qualify *Commonwealth v. Hunt* as the baseline decision for the American law of trade unionism. One involved the question of power, which, as Shaw noted, indubitably was why workers associated in unions.[32] Critical to everything else was his rejection of injury to others as a sufficient test of criminal conspiracy. Suppose a group of neighbors, victimized by the high price of bread, induced a rival baker to set up shop:

> The effect would be to diminish the profit of the former baker, and to the same extent impoverish him. And it might be said and proved, that the purpose of the associates was to diminish his profits, and thus impoverish him, though the ultimate and laudable object of the combination was to reduce the cost of bread to themselves and their neighbors. The same thing may be said of all competition in every branch of trade and industry; and yet it is through that competition, that the best interests of trade and industry are promoted.[33]

Trade unions, Shaw was suggesting, fell within this competitive ambit, striving for ends in themselves laudable (including, specifically, higher wages, a point Shaw made by dictum because no wage demand was involved in *Commonwealth v. Hunt*) but using means that, as in all marketplace competition, might have impoverishing consequences for others. The crucial test had to do with the means. If criminal by force or fraud, or unlawful by violating the legal rights of others, then a union might "be stamped with the character of conspiracy."[34] But so would any other association, and that was the crucial point, normalizing trade unions as economic actors and treating them like any other combination in an enterprising society that presumed that progress sprang from the clash of competing interests.[35]

Second, *Commonwealth v. Hunt* was a lodestar for what it had to say about free labor and, more specifically, about the balance Shaw struck between the liberties of the individual worker and the interests of the group. *Commonwealth v. Hunt* was deeply, one might say peculiarly, infused by the terms of free labor. This had, first, to do with the facts of the case, which arose from the complaint by a journeyman, Jeremiah Horne, that he had been deprived of employment by the action of the Boston bootmakers' society. Compulsion of his employer, Jeremiah Wait, was actually not at issue because Wait testified that, although he "did not feel at liberty to employ any but society men," he had not been "injured or oppressed" by the union's demand and, on the contrary, was the beneficiary of the good workmanship and steady habits inculcated by the union. He had, in fact, done his best to persuade Horne to make his peace with the bootmakers' society. Nor had Horne evidently suffered material injury because he had found other work at one of the smaller shops where the closed shop was not enforced. So, to a peculiar degree, *Commonwealth v. Hunt* was about his freedom to work.[36]

As for Shaw, he framed his opinion very much within those same free-labor terms. Thus, he noted, "It would have been a very different case" had the indictment stated "that Wait was under obligation, by contract, for an unexpired term of time, to employ and pay Horne."[37] Inducing a breach of contract would have caused Shaw to find against the bootmakers' society. It was likewise a free-labor perspective that informed Shaw's crucial distinction between American and English standards for conspiracy indictments. He trod familiar ground here. The acceptance of English law after the Revolution had always excepted what was unsuited to republican states. But consider his examples: "all those laws of the parent country" regulating wages, settling paupers, and enforcing apprenticeship—all, of course, laws inappropriate to a land of free labor.[38] Shaw, in fact, was bent on determining a law of collective action that was appropriate to a land of free labor.

"The case supposes that these persons are not bound by contract, but free to work for whom they please, or not work, if they so prefer. In this state of things, we cannot perceive, that it is criminal for men to agree together to exercise their own acknowledged rights, in such a manner as best to subserve their own interests," including by an agreement "that when they were free to act, they would not engage with an employer, or continue in his employment, if such an employer, when free to act, should engage with a workman, or continue a workman in his employment, not a member of the association."[39] At this point the circle closed between free labor and union power, for what justified privileging the bootmakers' society over the journeyman Horne was that the association needed "to induce all those engaged in the same occupation to become members of it" so as to gain the power to carry out its laudable purposes.

Questions of Power

The Boston bootmakers' society that Chief Justice Shaw had acquitted was an informal local body still rooted in the artisanal world of preindustrial America. Its postbellum successors, however, seemed far less benign, linked as they were into a nationalizing trade union movement and endowed with ever more formidable resources for battling employers. On another front, meanwhile, the Knights of Labor were developing a potent capacity for organizing on a community and industrywide basis. In the 1880s, as Knights' assemblies and craft unions grew prodigiously, a wave of strikes swept the country. A new tactic, the boycott, suddenly emerged, mobilizing labor's power against "unfair" employers with devastating effect and sparking a wave of sympathy strikes. To judges in their courtrooms, the boycott seemed like the opening gun of social revolution—"a reign of terror, which, if not checked and punished in the beginning by the law, will speedily and inevitably run into violence . . . and mob tyranny."[40]

In this crisis, what *Commonwealth v. Hunt* had achieved came undone. The labor boycott was of that class of acts, like a conspiracy to seduce a minor female, so "destructive of the happiness of individuals and the well being of society" as to justify proscription even in the absence of an applicable statute or common law offense. Thus, in *State v. Stewart*, one of several defining state appellate rulings of the mid-1880s, the Vermont Supreme Court declared itself not bound to find criminal conspiracy only when labor combinations "promote[d] objects or adopt[ed] means that [were] *per se* indictable." It was enough that the ends promoted or means employed be *"per se* oppressive, immoral or wrongfully prejudicial to the rights of others."[41] Presuming labor's actions to be uniquely ruinous of the public interest, the courts discarded what had been fundamental in *Commonwealth v. Hunt*, namely, that union power was in law indistinguishable from the power exerted by any other combination, or, as a major textbook put it in 1880, that "[we] cannot indict employees who combine, without indicting capitalists who combine."[42]

The courts had little trouble, of course, distinguishing capitalists from workers when it came to actions on the ground. Under the rubric of criminal means, a ready instrument was at hand for redefining the limits of permissible conduct during strikes and boycotts. The contrast with Britain is especially exact here because in both countries laws were enacted against the expansive court reading of criminal means. In Britain, however, "molestation" and "obstruction" gave way in 1875 to statutorily specified strike offenses, thereby ending judicial discretion in this realm.[43] In America, the anticonspiracy laws of Pennsylvania and New York never overrode the authority of the courts to decide what "intimidation" meant. The results are evident in the judge's instructions to the jury in the prosecution of New York bakery strikers in 1886. Regarding circulars, did they "contain appeals to the passions or are otherwise inflammatory"; in the absence of direct threats, did strikers maintain "an attitude of intimidation"; or might their numbers be taken to be intimidating? Any one of these would suffice for a conviction (and, as happened in this case, ten to thirty days in jail).[44] What emerged was a remarkable case law of strike conduct, distinct from the criminal code and aiming at "a species of intimidation that works upon the mind rather than the body [and is] quite as dangerous, and generally altogether more effective, than acts of actual violence."[45]

On a second front, the courts swept out the defenses set forth in *Commonwealth v. Hunt* for the exercise of trade union power. Thus, in *State v. Donaldson* (1867), the originating case in the postbellum generation of conspiracy prosecutions, the judge saw only "the purpose of oppression and mischief," whereas on the same showing of facts (save the employer's receptiveness) *Hunt* had seen a lawful union effort to strengthen itself.[46]

By demanding the dismissal of nonunion workers, the union was seeking to control the employer's business. This was the crux of it—that unions had no lawful right to strengthen themselves by what the courts defined as injury to or interference with an employer's business. In *State v. Glidden* (1887), arising from a boycott to oust nonunion printers from a Connecticut newspaper, the judge rejected the defendants' claim that they intended only to better their own conditions. Whatever their ultimate purpose, he ruled, their "direct and primary object must be regarded as the destruction of the [newspaper's] business."[47]

The final assault on *Hunt's* formulation came from the pen of William Howard Taft in *Moores v. Bricklayers' Union* (1889). Injury to others, Taft acknowledged, resulted whenever economic actors competed, but unions differed from other competitors because, in the unions' case, the injury done was "without cause or excuse" and hence showed malice. "The remote motive of wishing to better their condition by the power so acquired, will not . . . make any legal justification."[48]

Swift and mighty as this judicial response was, it did not, in fact, provide timely protection of boycotted employers. The situation was very like Britain's a century earlier, when common-law conspiracy had also proved wanting against an aroused working class. But where British authorities had turned to Parliament for summary justice via the Combination acts, their American successors only reached deeper into the bag of common law for the right instrument. This was the injunction, a restraining order issued by an equity court to provide a remedy where no adequate relief was available at law. Injunctions could be granted instantly at the court's discretion, and, as an initial order, they required no hearing or even notice to the affected persons. But such restraining orders, issuing from equity proceedings, applied only in very limited, well-specified circumstances, namely, repeated trespass or irreparable damage to real property.

Undeterred, the courts expanded the definition of protected property to encompass the business enterprise in its entirety and all its activities, with strikers "clearly trespassers" by virtue of the disruptions they
caused to business operations.[49] Within a few years, and with scant regard for precedent, the courts manufactured a new law of the labor injunction, driven by the conviction that, without pushing aside long-set-
tled rules of equity, the boycotted employer "is certainly remediless,
because an action at law, in most cases, would do no good, and ruin would
be accomplished before an adjudication would be reached."[50]

The impact was simply devastating. The injunction abruptly halt-
ed the boycott drive and, beyond that, disrupted what might have been
America's one chance to build a working-class movement comparable
to those taking shape in Europe. So potent was the injunction, in fact,
that it effectively replaced criminal proceedings in labor disputes. Conspiracy doctrine remained good law, but after the mid-1890s it was su-
perseded by summary restraining orders, which had undertaken the law's
work of suppressing strikes and boycotts done—in the new language of
labor conspiracy—with "a malicious intent to injure and destroy the
complainant's business."[51]

The labor injunction was also the bridge by which federal courts joined
the legal assault on trade unionism. They had, in fact, been the first courts
to use labor injunctions, initially to shield railroads in receivership (and
hence court-controlled) from strikes; then, with the Interstate Commerce
Act (1887), against railroad strikes more generally as obstructions of commerce; and, finally, against strikes and boycotts construed to be conspiracies in restraint of trade under the Sherman Antitrust Act (1890). In the
great Pullman boycott of 1894 the federal injunction was unveiled in all
its might, immobilizing the strike officers and sending their leader, Eugene
V. Debs, to prison for contempt of court.

From this point onward, moreover, state and federal jurisdictions
increasingly overlapped, with federal courts holding that they could,
under the diverse citizenship provision of the Constitution, entertain
labor cases even absent a federal violation if the parties were citizens
of different states. All it took was an out-of-state third party (conniv-
ing of course with the "defendant" employer) coming forward with a
claim to a material interest in the dispute. So advantageous did the federal jurisdiction prove to be that over the next thirty years roughly two-
thirds of all labor cases, mostly of local provenance, came to federal
courts.[52]

The labor movement was cast down, to use William Forbath's apt
phrase, into "semi-outlawry":

An injunction against picketing could vanquish a strike, but for every picket line enjoined, many more were broken up without court decisions by local officials who invoked the illegality of picketing, boycotts, organizing, and closed-shop strikes. The courts had woven a powerful web of associations between strikers' use of economic "coercion" and their use of brute physical force, between popular images of criminal conspirators and the legal construction of virtually all secondary actions as conspiracies in restraint of trade, and between picketing in any fashion and threats of violence.[53]

The victory was, in a sense, too complete. "Defy the law," a union leader urged a mass meeting of striking Chicago printers in 1905. "Judge-made law is not good law." In its distress, the embattled American Federation of Labor was driven onto the path of civil disobedience. "Contempt of court" is "obedience to law," proclaimed Samuel Gompers, who showed himself as good as his word by defying the *Buck's Stove* injunction and courting a year in jail.[54] The precious consent that law required thus jeopardized, the courts sought to shore up by appealing to that other strand of *Commonwealth v. Hunt*—the law of free labor.

The Utility of Free Labor

The conspiracy decisions of the 1880s sometimes proscribed combinations "designed to coerce workmen to become members, or to interfere with, obstruct, vex, or annoy them in working, or in obtaining work, because they are not members, or in order to induce them to become members."[55] From this reading sprang a minor line of case law establishing the right of a discharged worker to sue for damages—as, for example, an engineer did after being ousted from his job because of a closed-shop agreement between the brewery union and an employers' association. The New York Court of Appeals found in his favor, ruling in *Curran v. Galen* (1897) that he had been unlawfully deprived of his "constitutional right freely to pursue a lawful avocation, under conditions equal as to all."[56] But that right was ringed by limitations—by whether, for example, he could have joined the union had he so chosen or whether other suitable work was to be had—and seems rarely to have been asserted by aggrieved nonunion workers. *Curran* was reversed in 1905.[57] The paramount legal issue was not whether the closed shop violated the rights of nonunion workers but whether the closed shop had the assent of the employer.

This was the crux of the matter, and, for practical purposes, so it had been ever since the revival of conspiracy law after the Civil War. The language of *State v. Donaldson* (1867), the first important conspiracy case to surface after *Hunt,* is telling on that score. The closed shop that the defendants sought "cannot in any event be advantageous to the employee" but "must always be hurtful to the employer," who "in the presence of a coalition of his employees . . . must submit."[58] Later judges knew better than to privilege the employer's rights in this bald way, but that, in fact, was where the law had real bite—that when workers "combine . . . to prevent an employer from employing others by threats of a strike, they combine to accomplish an unlawful purpose."[59]

The closed shop was, in reality, preeminently about power relations. Listen, for example, to Abraham Bisno, a "walking delegate" for the Chicago garment workers: "We could not have an organization at all unless we had an organization that was competent to protect the individual member from being thrown out of employment for being a union man. . . . So when these men demand that the union be recognized to the extent of employing no other people except members of their union, this is essential to the very existence of their organization. It is a life-and-death question with them."[60]

And so, on the other side, it was with employers. By resisting the closed shop they resisted collective bargaining. What the landmark conspiracy cases of the 1880s mainly vindicated was the employer's interest in a struggle over unionization, not the rights of individual workers in deference to the law of free labor. Where their individual rights did hugely figure was as ideology, as I have defined it, an imagined world of free and equal workers. Thus, in an 1887 debate on the tumultuous labor crisis, it was Colorado senator Henry Teller's conviction that

> [N]o laboring man for a moment should surrender [the right of free contract], either to the State, to his fellow-workmen, or to capital. His labor is valuable to him only as it is at his uncontrolled disposal, both as to whom he will sell it, and when he will sell it. Any interference by his fellow workmen of the same trade or any other in the disposal of his labor is an invasion of his right. . . . The difference between a slave and a freeman consists mainly in the fact that the freeman may freely dispose of his labor . . . on the terms fixed by himself.[61]

The labor conspiracy cases are replete with this language of free labor, going back, indeed, to the very first, when, having described how Philadelphia shoemakers disciplined their ranks, Moses Levy burst out indignantly, "Is this freedom? Is it not restraining, instead of promoting the Spirit of '76?"[62]

Then and long after, Levy's republican cry of freedom encompassed the self-employed as well as wage workers. In the *Slaughter-House Cases* (1873), Forbath reminds us, Justice Stephen J. Field invoked "the right of free labor" on behalf of New Orleans butcher-entrepreneurs against a state-mandated stockyards monopoly. But while Field's dissent eventually became ruling doctrine, his invocation of free labor in defense of entrepreneurial rights fell silent and, Forbath finds, played no part in the succeeding line of due-process cases restraining the states' regulation of business. With the rise of a permanent working class, the language was no longer of the free laborers' right to "the fruits of their labor" but only of their freedom to sell their labor to "those who might be disposed to employ them."[63]

In conspiracy cases, the essential task was to enfold this hard truth within the law's repressive project, first by invoking the glories of freedom of contract in which "every owner of property may work it as he will, by whom he pleases, at such wages, and upon such terms as he can make; and every laborer may work or not, as he sees fit, for whom, and at such wages as, he pleases; and neither can dictate to the other how he shall use his own, whether of property, time, or skill."[64] The second part of the task was to use the elastic definition of property (everything of "exchange value") now taking hold generally in American jurisprudence and vividly voiced, for example, by *State v. Stewart:* "The labor and skill of the workman, be it of high or low degree, the plant of the manufacturer, the equipment of the farmer, the investments of commerce, are all in equal sense property." All were equally to be protected from "the anathemas of secret organization of men combined for the purpose of controlling the industry of others."[65]

How free-labor ideology, so formulated, was mobilized against "the anathema of secret organizations" is best seen in the work of the American Anti-Boycott Association (AABA), which was formed in 1903 by two Danbury hat manufacturers threatened by a union boycott. By this time, boycotting strategy had entered a new, more sophisticated phase, operating through a nationwide trade union network and targeting unfair employers in multiple local markets. The AABA's purpose was to defend this class of threatened firms by spreading the costs of litigation and developing the legal expertise to challenge the boycott. The undertaking ended triumphantly in *Loewe v. Lawlor* (1908), which declared "We Don't Patronize" campaigns to be conspiracies in restraint of trade under the Sherman Act (and subjected the Danbury members to triple damages). The economic roots of this case were in the cutthroat soft-hat market, pitting the marginal operator Loewe against the Hatters' Union and its campaign to take wages out of competition and stabilize the industry. The closed-shop clause was, in Loewe's case, not exactly incidental because some employees evidently stood to lose their places if he signed the contract, but his decision to fight the union was dictated by his situation as a low-wage competitor.

Audiences could scarcely have drawn that conclusion. The AABA presented itself as champion of the open shop, cloaked in the Declaration of Independence and standing for "the free rights of every American citizen." The closed shop had to be resisted, said the AABA attorney Daniel Davenport, because "every man, I don't care who he is, has implanted in his heart the deep seated love of liberty." Davenport inveighed against trade unionists for excluding "others from the opportunity to work, although those others are of the same condition in life as themselves and have nothing but their hands and their dexterity by which to live and support their families." To drive home his point, Davenport described the abuse of a respectable young woman ("any man would have been proud to call her sister or daughter") who had tried to go to work during the recent Chicago packinghouse strike of 1904. "They seized that girl, they rolled her in the mud, they disfigured her, and they subjected her person to indignities not fit to be described in your presence." The incident had made Davenport's "blood boil."[66]

In our postmodernist age, historians are disinclined to be skeptical of such pronouncements or, at any rate, to regard them as true as anything else that is said or written. So it may bear mentioning that the one great case in which the law of free labor did figure centrally—*Commonwealth v. Hunt*—was devoid of the cant of free-labor dogma. Indeed, what most provoked Chief Justice Shaw were the "qualifying epithets (as 'unlawful, deceitful, pernicious,' &c.)" larding the indictment and the partisan bent of the lower-court proceedings.[67]

Had employers wanted to make the law of free labor determining, they only had to heed Shaw's advice and sign their employees to time contracts. This, however, they declined to do, far preferring the freedom of at-will employment and content with the legal protections they already enjoyed. To this generalization, one exception stands out.

From the 1870s onward, many firms required workers to sign "iron-clads" (better known, in later years, as yellow-dog contracts) stating that, as a condition of employment, they would not join a union. The yellow-dog was a good contract, consistently upheld by the courts against state laws seeking to declare it illegal. But for many years the effect was strictly atmospheric inasmuch as, in practice, the employer's only recourse against breach of contract was discharge (which was his absolute right anyway).[68] In 1907, however, the Hitchman Coal and Coke Company bethought itself to seek an injunction on the grounds that the organizing activity of the United Mine Workers amounted to inducing breach of contract by its miners. When the Supreme Court finally upheld the company's application in 1917, freedom of contract and the injunction fused into an extraordinary defense against unionization. The Court justified its decision on familiar free-labor grounds:

> The same liberty which enables men to form unions, and through the union to enter into agreements with employers willing to agree, entitles other men to remain independent of the union and other employers to agree with them to employ no man who owes any allegiance or obligation to the union. . . . Plaintiff, having in the exercise of its undoubted rights established a working agreement between it and its employees, with the free assent of the latter, is entitled to be protected in the resulting status, as in any other legal right.[69]

Out in the coalfields where nonunion contracts proliferated (and acquired their "yellow dog" designation), operators boasted that they were upholding "a principle of democracy." Miners, if they bothered to read the contracts they were signing, would have seen that they were affirming "the preservation of the right of individual contract, free from interference or regulation by others, and payment in proportion to service."[70]

In 1927 *W.M.W.A. v. Red Jacket* upheld an injunction that effectively ordered the United Mine Workers away from all of southern West Virginia, a district of forty thousand miners. The presiding circuit court judge, John J. Parker, paid for *Red Jacket* by forfeiting his elevation to the Supreme Court three years later. In the Senate confirmation battle, Judge Parker had many defenders (and the defense that he was bound by *Hitchman*), but only one senator defended the yellow-dog contract. It was, in fact, indefensible. And the judicial system, for defending it, suffered a remarkable moral collapse. The courts had overreached themselves.

The Imprint of the Old Order

On March 23, 1932, Congress passed the Norris-LaGuardia Anti-Injunction Act. Norris-LaGuardia declared the yellow-dog contract unenforceable in federal courts and denied them authority to issue injunctions in most labor disputes. For the well-specified exceptions, the law laid down rigorous procedural and evidentiary protections. Norris-LaGuardia was an act of demolition, sweeping out the worst of judge-made labor law and preparing the ground for a new regime of statutory labor relations. Norris-LaGuardia took note of "the aid of governmental authority for owners of property to organize in the corporate and other forms of ownership association." Because of the resulting imbalance, "the individual worker is commonly helpless to exercise actual liberty of contract and to protect his freedom of labor, and thereby to obtain acceptable terms and conditions of employment." These were remarkable words, recapitulating *Commonwealth v. Hunt's* disdain for the unequal legal treatment of capital and labor but now marshaling the language of free labor more forcefully on behalf of solidarity. "Under prevailing economic conditions," said Norris-LaGuardia, workers will want to act collectively because only in that way can they exercise "actual freedom of contract."

In the National Labor Relations [Wagner] Act of 1935, what Norris-LaGuardia asserted in principle received the force of law. The heart of the Wagner Act was Section 7, declaring the rights of workers to organize and bargain collectively through representatives of their own choosing. Section 8 enforced those rights. Employers could not interfere with, restrain, or coerce employees; dominate or interfere with labor organizations; discriminate against employees to discourage union membership; or refuse to bargain with representatives of their employees.

The law might have stopped at this point—Norris-LaGuardia had contemplated nothing further—but for the stormy labor history of the early New Deal's National Recovery Administration, out of which came the decision that the state had to take charge of the process for setting collective bargaining in motion. The result was a preferred bargaining structure based on "exclusive representation"—one union for all the workers in a plant or other "appropriate" unit—and the principle of majority rule in the choice by workers of representatives, with whom the employers had a duty to bargain.

In its time, the Wagner Act was celebrated (or, alternately, reviled) as the most radical law of the New Deal era. Its passage helped spark the greatest surge of labor organizing in American history. Formidable industrial unions emerged; millions of workers joined; and, in the postwar era, collective bargaining became a national institution governing the labor relations of the booming industrial economy. At its height in the mid-1950s, organized labor represented eighteen million workers, a third of the entire American labor force. In such basic industries as steel, automobiles, and mining, union coverage was virtually total. But slowly, and then precipitously as the economy foundered in the 1970s, unions lost ground until in the private sector they stand today roughly where they did before the New Deal, with scarcely one worker in ten a union member.

The law, it turns out, is not what it seemed. We can track its impotence in the rising incidence of unfair labor practice charges against employers, which amounted to a few thousand a year in the mid-1950s but

thirty-five thousand in 1980; or in the failure rate of unions in representation elections, which rose above 50 percent, notwithstanding that unions
almost never petition for an election without signed cards from a good
majority of those they seek to represent; or in the fact that, when they do
prevail, unions fail one time in three to get a first contract, notwithstanding that the law requires the employer to bargain in good faith with them.[71]
Workers are fired every day for union activities, and nonunion workers
know it. In a Harris poll, 43 percent of workers in a sample believed that
they would be fired if they joined a union. A Wilson Center survey found
that only 24 percent thought that their employer would "let the employees decide on their own."[72] Had such polls been taken before the advent
of the Wagner Act, the results would likely not have been far different. In
that convergence of past and present, I find my concluding text, for what
I want to argue is the staying power of the old order and its imprint, only
now fully visible, on the failing collective-bargaining law of our own time.

It might have seemed, in such a law, that claims of solidarity would
take precedence. That, most certainly, was what the authors of the Wagner Act had intended. We can see their hand, for example, in the omis-
sion from the law's Section 7 rights of the right of workers (acknowledged
in original Norris-LaGuardia language) not to associate; in the provision
that, once a majority selected a bargaining agent, every worker in the unit
had to accept representation by that agent; and in the absence of any ac-
knowledgment that workers might be coerced by labor organizations.
More fundamental was "self-organization"—first of the Section 7 rights—
which the law's authors intended as the doctrinal underpinning for the
solidaristic bent of the law. For a heady time it seemed as if they had solved
the riddle of freedom and solidarity. Workers were free, but they would
express that freedom collectively and reap the benefits of "actual freedom
of contract." A labor law based on that premise would surely bring forth
a great and powerful union movement. And, for one generation, it did.

Then, with the sweeping Taft-Hartley amendments of 1947, the hard
truth set in, signaled by the reinsertion in Section 7 of the worker's right
"to refrain from any and all [concerted] activities."[73] From this language
followed the "right-to-work" provision in the amended law. The Wagner
Act expressly permitted the union shop where it derived from an agreement between the employer and a union with standing as exclusive bargaining agent. Now, in Section 14(b), Taft-Hartley invited the states to
exempt themselves from that provision. In right-to-work states, nonunion
workers acquired stronger rights of nonassociation than they had ever
enjoyed under the pre–New Deal legal regime because in no circumstances (not even by the assent of their employers) could they now be

required to join a union. More remarkable, although less noticed, was Taft-Hartley's assault on the law's conception of self-organization, which was done procedurally by making the representation election mandatory for certification and substantively by withdrawing the privileged status of labor organizations in the exercise of workers' rights. The mandated collective-bargaining structure was not altered nor, despite fierce denunciations by the labor movement, was the unionized sector visibly damaged. Taft-Hartley was craftier, striking not at the edifice of collective bargaining but at the sustaining premises of solidarity. In that endeavor it succeeded, setting in motion in the name of individual rights and free choice the corrosive forces that ate away at the law and rendered it in our own time an empty bulwark of labor's collective rights.

Taft-Hartley was a political event, and in that sense it was fixed in the chronology of the postwar reaction against the New Deal. The Republicans, having retaken the Congress in 1946, had the votes to pass Taft-Hartley and override President Truman's veto. But, in concept, Taft-Hartley was the Wagner Act's relentless companion from the first.[74] Scores of congressional bills (not to mention hostile hearings) preceded Taft-Hartley. It was only a matter of time, and the right political conditions, before Taft-Hartley or something very like it would prevail. The Wagner Act was vulnerable to Taft-Hartley from birth, and here too, in its vulnerability, we find the imprint of the old order.

On the main question—the worker's right to organize—the Supreme Court had long since taken its stand. The lead case was *Adair v. U.S.* (1908), declaring unconstitutional a provision of the Erdman Act (1898) that forbade railroads from discharging employees for union membership. *Adair* rested squarely on liberty of contract and its companion, free labor. "The right of the employee to quit the service of the employer, for whatever reason, is the same as the right of the employer, for whatever reason, to dispense with the services of such employee. . . . Any legislation that disturbs that equality is an arbitrary interference with liberty of contract which no government can justify in a free land."[75] *Adair* served, in turn, as the legal grounding for the yellow-dog contract.

Everyone in labor's camp agreed on the vileness of the yellow-dog contract but not about how to kill it. AFL leaders wanted a frontal attack that challenged *Adair*'s espousal of liberty of contract and seized the banner of free labor for their own cause. They assailed the yellow-dog contract as "fully as destructive of human liberty as a condition of peonage," conducive of "economic servitude" and, altogether, "as un-American as peonage or slavery."[76] Legal experts, citing the failed rights language of the Clayton Anti-Trust Act (1914), demurred. They regarded *Adair* as authoritative. Rather than being declared illegal because (as the AFL argued) it violated the worker's freedom, the yellow-dog contract became merely unenforceable, and the injunction, rather than being declared inapplicable to labor disputes because (as the AFL argued) labor was not property, became restricted. Norris-LaGuardia was high legislative craft but witness also to an insurmountable case law. In the estimation of Norris-LaGuardia's authors the rights-based act that the AFL wanted would never have prevailed against *Adair*.

The Wagner Act, however, required a different maneuver inasmuch as it met *Adair* head-on. The solution was supplied by Oliver Wendell Holmes Jr., who in his dissent to *Adair* had argued that the employer's liberty was not being fundamentally challenged. Protecting union workers from discrimination constituted "in substance, a very limited interference with freedom of contract, no more."[77] So, still less, did the interference by the Wagner Act because the law that Mr. Justice Holmes was defending had made discharge of union workers a criminal offense. In the Wagner Act, it was only an unfair labor practice, the remedy for which was, in discharge cases, reemployment with back pay (minus interim earnings) and, on other violations, an NLRB order to cease and desist and, where appropriate, restore the status quo.

At the time, of course, the legislative drafters of the act had in mind the urgent business of getting it past the Supreme Court, which they did, to the general consternation of conservatives, in *NLRB v. Jones and Laughlin* (1937). They were content that *Adair* be left intact (as it remains to this day, still authoritative on at-will employment) and that their law be excepted from *Adair*.

The Court's exact words were that *Adair* was "inapplicable to legislation of this character."[78] Here, too, the hand of Mr. Justice Holmes could be seen. If, on "an important ground of public policy" Congress chose to intrude on liberty of contract, "the Constitution does not forbid it, whether this court agrees or disagrees with the policy pursued."[79] Holmes was the high priest of legal realism, and in *Adair* he was striking a blow at judicial formalism. Following Holmes, New Deal progressives regarded a labor law not grounded in inalienable rights as a positive achievement. Far better that it be re-centered, as their mentor had said in *Vegelahn v. Guntner* (1896), on "considerations of policy and social advantage."

Norris-LaGuardia, in fact, had done just that. It curbed the yellow-dog contract and labor injunction because they were contrary to "public policy," which was that workers not be denied the benefits of collective bargaining. In the Wagner Act, the affirmation of collective bargaining became more assertive. Its practice and procedure were to be "encouraged," in part because this was what the constitutional argument for the law demanded—collective bargaining reduced the industrial strife that obstructed interstate commerce—and in part because the Great Depression had brought forth an economic rationale for collective bargaining. Its absence "tends to aggravate recurrent business depressions, by depressing wage rates and the purchasing power of wage earners in industry and by preventing the stabilization of competitive wage rates and working conditions within and between industries."

These propositions, remnants of early New Deal corporatism, are still in the labor law, but no politician would dream of espousing them in our globalized, free-market age. Nor, in broader terms, does public policy today, or for the quarter-century past, actually correspond to the declared policy of the labor law that collective bargaining is good for the country. Thus, if we look at how the law today works rather than at what it professes, a "union-free environment" has as much legitimacy as—and, in fact, holds a decided advantage over—collective bargaining. At the law's nadir in the Reagan era, the NLRB chair himself was heard to say that "collective bargaining frequently means monopoly, the destruction of the marketplace."[80] It may have been quixotic, as legal realists believed, for the AFL to prefer a labor law grounded in the inalienable rights of free labor, but the alternative has been a labor law grounded only in the shifting sands of public policy.

In the old days, a key word in labor's vocabulary had been "recognition." It referred to the standing a union attained on entering contractual relations with an employer. In granting recognition, the employer acknowledged the union's power. Overtly or not, the process leading to collective bargaining constituted a power struggle. The primary function of labor law was to police this struggle, which it did, as we have seen, with unabashed and ultimately reckless disregard for labor's side. With the advent of the Wagner Act, the key word became "certification," meaning a union's official standing as exclusive bargaining agent (and the employer's correlative obligation to negotiate with it). This was the essence of the New Deal's collective-bargaining revolution. The state had undertaken to replace equations of power with a rule of law, which consisted, of course, of the provisions of the Wagner Act. So long as employers consented, the revolution held, but once they regrouped and counterattacked, the fragility of that rule of law stood forth, and so, I am suggesting, did the imprint of the old legal regime. By centering itself, as it had to do, on the rights of workers, the modern labor law was reproducing the free-labor premises of the old regime and hence reproducing, within its own confines, the abiding American tension between freedom and solidarity.

No trade unionist would want to return to the days of yellow-dog contracts and wholesale labor injunctions. But the evil that they did at least had the virtue of clarity. The oppression of workers today is mostly invisible, masked within the processes of a law that speaks in the language of labor's rights. The labor movement has demanded reform for many years, but as the more fundamental problems in the law have emerged it has become less apparent just how to deal with them. In any case, the weakened movement lacks the necessary political clout to reform the law. In the meantime, some unions are beginning to vote with their feet. They are boycotting NLRB elections, organizing workers directly, and pressuring employers for voluntary recognition. In acting in an old-fashioned way, of course, they are inviting an old-fashioned response, which now includes even a revival of labor conspiracy via a federal racketeering law that the courts have begun to apply against vigorously fought strikes.[81]

All of this suggests an unstable future for the collective bargaining law. But there is nothing unstable about the underlying dynamics that, ever since the earliest craft unions, rendered the law of labor a burden on American trade unionism. It would be implausible, of course, to attribute the failure of the modern labor law to an obscure Indiana decision back in 1821 declaring that a woman of color, Mary Clark, could not be held to her indenture because that constituted involuntary servitude. Yet the free-labor doctrine embraced by *Mary Clark*, unimpeachable though it be, is also surely implicated in the peculiar disfavor in which the claims of solidarity are held, even in a law whose declared purpose is the encouragement of collective bargaining.

Notes

1. A. V. Dicey, *Lectures on the Relation between Law and Public Opinion in England during the Nineteenth Century*, 2d ed. (London, 1930), 468.

2. Richard B. Morris, *Government and Labor in Early America* (New York, 1946).

3. C. B. MacPherson, *The Political Theory of Possessive Individualism: Hobbes to Locke* (New York, 1964), 142.

4. Robert J. Steinfeld, *The Invention of Free Labor: The Employment Relation in English and American Law and Culture, 1350–1870* (Chapel Hill, 1991), 92.

5. Steinfeld, *The Invention of Free Labor*, 47–51.

6. Ibid., ch. 5.

7. Robert J. Goldstein, *Political Repression in Nineteenth-Century Europe* (London, 1983), 58–59.

8. Jürgen Kocka, "Problems of Working-Class Formation in Germany: The Early Years, 1800–1875," in *Working-Class Formation: Nineteenth-Century Patterns in Western Europe and the United States*, ed. Ira Katznelson and Aristide R. Zolberg (Princeton, 1986), 312–13.

9. Steinfeld, *The Invention of Free Labor*, 102.

10. Ibid., 139–41.

11. Ibid., 156 (quoted).

12. Henry Williams in *Official Report of the Debates and Proceedings . . . to Revise and Amend the Constitution of the Commonwealth of Massachusetts* (Boston, 1853), 550.

13. For a stimulating exploration of the linkage between suffrage and free labor, see Robert J. Steinfeld, "Property and Suffrage in the Early American Republic," *Stanford Law Review* 41 (Jan. 1989): 335–76.

14. Steinfeld, "Property and Suffrage," 550.

15. Ibid., 574–78.

16. Goldstein, *Political Repression*, 58; a survey of European trade-union restrictions appears in table 2.2. on page 56.

17. Gary Marks, *Unions in Politics: Britain, Germany and the United States in the Nineteenth and Early Twentieth Centuries* (Princeton, 1989), 56.

18. Christopher L. Tomlins, *Law, Labor, and Ideology in the Early American Republic* (New York, 1993), 99.

19. *Commonwealth v. Pulis* (1806), in *A Documentary History of American Industrial Society*, ed. John R. Commons et al., 10 vols. (Cleveland, 1910) 3:59–248 (hereafter *Documentary History*). Citations to the scholarly commentary on *Commonwealth v. Pulis* are found in Tomlins, *Law, Labor, and Ideology*, 107–8n1.

20. Commons et al., eds., *Documentary History*, 3:232–33.

21. Ibid., 3:234.

22. Tomlins, *Law, Labor and Ideology*, 134–35.

23. Commons et al., eds., *Documentary History*, 3:224–25, 3:231–32.

24. Tomlims, *Law, Labor and Ideology*. In a more spacious way, see David Montgomery, *Citizen Worker: The Experience of Workers in the United States with Democracy and the Free Market during the Nineteenth Century* (New York, 1993).

25. This is a main theme of Victoria C. Hattam, *Labor Visions and State Power: The Origins of Business Unionism in the United States* (Princeton, 1993), chs. 4, 5. For Britain's diverging history, in which Parliament seized control of the labor law from the courts, see especially John V. Orth, *Combination and Conspiracy: A Legal History of Trade Unionism, 1721–1906* (Oxford, 1991).

26. *People v. Melvyn* (N.Y. 1809), in *Documentary History*, 3:385.

27. For a survey of these cases, see Tomlins, *Law, Labor and Ideology*, chap. 5.

28. 45 Mass. 111.

29. Ibid., 128–29.

30. Ibid., 123.

31. Walter Nelles, "Commonwealth v. Hunt," *Columbia Law Review* 32 (Nov. 1932): 1149.

32. *Commonwealth v. Hunt*, 129.

33. Ibid., 134.

34. Ibid.

35. On this point, see especially Leonard W. Levy, *The Law of the Commonwealth and Chief Justice Shaw* (Cambridge, 1957), 202–6.

36. These details first came to light in Nelles, "Commonwealth v. Hunt," 1131–38.

37. *Commonwealth v. Hunt*, 132.

38. Ibid., 122.

39. Ibid., 130–31.

40. *Crump v. Commonwealth*, 84 Va. 927 (1888), quoted in Haggai Hurvitz, "American Labor Law and the Doctrine of Entrepreneurial Property Rights . . . 1886–1895," *Industrial Relations Law Journal* 8, no. 3 (1986): 212.

41. *State v. Stewart*, 59 Vt. 273 (1887), quoted in Hurvitz, "American Labor Law," 324–25.

42. Quoted in Hurvitz, "American Labor Law," 321, whose argument I am following here.

43. Orth, *Combination and Conspiracy*, 143–44.

44. *People v. Kostka*, 4 N.Y. Crim. 403 (1886), in Hattam, *Labor Visons and State Power*, 147–48; see also Hyman Kuritz, "Criminal Conspiracy Cases in Post-Bellum Pennsylvania," *Pennsylvania History* 17 (Oct. 1950): 298–300.

45. *State v. Stewart*, quoted in Karen Orren, *Belated Feudalism: Labor, the Law, and Liberal Development in the United States* (New York, 1991), 130.

46. Chistopher Tomlins, *The State and the Unions: Labor Relations, Law, and the Organized Labor Movement in America, 1880–1960* (New York, 1985), 47.

47. 55 Conn. 46, in Daniel R. Ernst, *Lawyers against Labor: From Individual Rights to Corporate Liberalism* (Champaign, 1995), 73.

48. Hurvitz, "American Labor Law," 330–32.

49. *New York, Lake Erie and Western Railroad v. Wenger*, 9 Ohio Dec. Reprint 815 (1887), in Hurvitz, "American Labor Law," 341.

50. *Emack v. Kane*, 34 F. 46 (Ill. 1888), in Hurvitz, "American Labor Law," 338.

51. *Casey v. Cincinnati Typographical Union*, 45 F. 135 (Ohio 1891), in Hurvitz, "American Labor Law," 337–38.

52. Felix Frankfurter and Nathan Greene, *The Labor Injunction* (New York, 1930), 11–17, 210.

53. William Forbath, *Law and the Shaping of the American Labor Movement* (Cambridge, 1991), 126.

54. Forbath, *Law and the Shaping of the American Labor Movement*, 144–45.

55. *Old Dominion Steam-Ship Co. v. McKenna*, 30 F. 48 (N.Y. 1887), in Hurvitz, "American Labor Law," 329–30.

56. 52 N.Y. 33, 46 N.Y. 297 (1897), in Ernst, *Lawyers against Labor*, 93.

57. *Jacobs v. Cohen*, 183 N.Y. 207 (1905), in Charles O. Gregory, *Labor and the Law* (New York, 1949), 80.

58. Quoted in Tomlins, *State and the Unions*, 47.

59. *Erdman v. Mitchell*, 207 Pa. 79 (1903), in Orren, *Belated Feudalism*, 132.

60. Testimony, U.S. Industrial Commission, *Report* (1901), reprinted in *The Nation Transformed*, ed. Sigmund Diamond (New York, 1963), 194.

61. *Congressional Record*, 49th Cong., 2d sess. (1887), 2375–76, cited (and partially quoted) in Melvyn Dubofsky, *The State and Labor in Modern America* (Chapel Hill, 1994), 18–19.

62. Commons et al., eds., *Documentary History*, 3:235.

63. William E. Forbath, "The Ambiguities of Free Labor: Labor and Law in the Gilded Age," *Wisconsin Law Review* (1985): 772–73, 781–82.

64. *Coeur d'Alene Consolidated and Mining Co. v. Miners Union*, 51 F. 260 (Idaho 1892), in Hurvitz, "American Labor Law," 344.

65. Quoted in Tomlins, *State and the Unions,* 49.

66. Quotations in Ernst, *Lawyers against Labor,* 64–65.

67. *Commonwealth v. Hunt,* 111, 128.

68. After a thorough search, Joel D. Seidman, *The Yellow Dog Contract* (Baltimore, 1932), 37, finds no record of breach-of-contract suits against employees.

69. *Hitchman Coal and Coke Company v. Mitchell,* 247 U.S. 229 (1917), reprinted in *Cases in Labor Relations Law,* ed. Benjamin J. Taylor and Fred Witney (Englewood Cliffs, 1987), 12.

70. Quotation in Daniel Ernst, "The Yellow-Dog Contract and Liberal Reform, 1917–1932," *Labor History* 30 (Spring 1989): 258–59.

71. Paul C. Weiler, *Governing the Workplace: The Future of Labor and Employment Law* (Cambridge, 1990), ch. 3; Sheldon Friedman et al., eds., *Restoring the Promise of American Labor Law* (Ithaca, 1994), pt. 2.

72. Weiler, *Governing the Workplace,* 112–14; Friedman et al., eds., *Restoring the Promise of American Labor Law,* 98–99.

73. For an account especially stressing this change, see James A. Gross, *Broken Promises: The Subversion of U.S. Labor Relations Policy, 1947–1994* (Philadelphia, 1995).

74. See, for example, the statement of Walter Gordon Merritt in *Legislative History of the National Labor Relations Act, 1935,* 2 vols. (Washington, D.C., 1959), 1:1018–20.

75. 208 U.S. 161, repr. in *Labor Law: Cases: Text and Legislation,* ed. E. Edward Herman and Gordon S. Skinner (New York, 1972), 85–89.

76. Quotations in Ernst, "Yellow-Dog Contract," 263–65; Seidman, *Yellow-Dog Contract,* 31, 33. On the AFL's thinking, see the perceptive analysis in Forbath, *Law and the Shaping of the Labor Movement,* ch. 5.

77. *Adair v. U.S.,* in *Labor Law,* ed. Herman and Skinner, 89.

78. *NLRB v. Jones and Jones and Laughlin* (1937) 301 U.S. 1, repr. in *Labor Law,* ed. Herman and Skinner, 104.

79. *Adair v. U.S.,* in *Labor Law,* ed. Herman and Skinner, 89.

80. Donald Dotson, quoted in *Restoring the Promise,* ed. Friedman et al., 90.

81. David Brody, "Criminalizing the Rights of Labor," *Dissent* (Summer 1995): 363–67.

9   Labor's Rights: Finding a Way

The short essays that compose this final chapter exemplify applied labor history in unalloyed form. All three were prompted by specific events that crystalized an argument in my mind—the first by a bitter battle over collective-bargaining rights at the Avondale shipyards in Louisiana, the second by a Human Rights Watch report on workers' rights in the United States, and the third by the introduction of congressional legislation outlawing voluntary recognition of unions. In no case could I have written these essays without the groundwork laid in the preceding chapters. Accordingly, the reader will have to bear with a certain amount of repetition and, hopefully, be rewarded by an argument now applied to policy. I make no bones about it. In these essays, I am trying to tell the labor movement what to do.

A Question of Rights

Late in the summer of 1998, in the last days of the Supreme Court term, the press was awash with talk of the pending sexual harassment cases. The gist of this reportage was that employers urgently needed clarification about how to avoid being sued. So great was the risk of "ruinous liability," observed Jeffrey Rosen in *The New Republic*, that companies were tightening compliance programs to the point where free speech rights of employees at the workplace were in serious jeopardy.

In the midst of all this anxious talk, the *New York Times* carried one of its signature investigative reports, this one on the five-year union struggle for collective bargaining at the Avondale shipyards in New Orleans. The National Labor Relations Board found Avondale guilty of "egregious misconduct" and "an outrageous and pervasive number" of labor law violations, including the illegal dismissal of twenty-eight union workers. After four years the twenty-eight still await reinstatement.[1]

What the article neglected to mention was that companies that fire union workers don't really care whether years later the charges against them are upheld. The main thing is that they have meanwhile defeated the union and preserved their union-free environment. There's no penalty except reinstating the fired workers (providing they have the stomach to return) and giving them back pay (minus interim earnings). As for the burden of guilt, forget it. No shame attaches to violating the labor law.

An attentive *Times* reader might have wondered about the discrepancy—discriminating against workers because of gender is a big deal; discriminating against them for union membership is a joke. But why? After all, both are violations of federal law. Not all laws are created equal, of course. The sexual harassment cases arise from civil rights legislation with real bite, grounded in the Fifth and Fourteenth amendments. Where are we to find the foundations for the National Labor Relations Act?

In its 1937 decision validating the act, the Supreme Court asserted that workers had "a fundamental right" to organize and bargain collectively. And, yes, it is always inspiring to read the recitation in the act's Section 7—"the right to self-organization, to form, join, or assist labor organizations, to bargain collectively through representatives of their own choosing, or to engage in other concerted activities for the purpose of collective bargaining or other mutual aid or protection." If we start with these words, the weakness of the modern labor law has to be framed as a nullification, a betrayal. That, I hasten to say, has long been my view. But the occasion recently to read more widely in American labor law has persuaded me that we may be barking up the wrong tree. That is, rather than focusing on what's wrong with the current law, we might better begin by examining its legal and doctrinal foundations. What I want to argue is that the problems we have with the law are rooted in the original formulation of the Wagner Act. Furthermore, if we are to have meaningful reform we have first of all to come to grips with the legal history that has beset our modern labor law from the outset.

Historically, labor's freedom of association was a liberty not a state-protected right. Workers were free to organize and bargain collectively, but so were employers to fire them and reject any dealings with unions. The role of the state was to police this private struggle between labor and capital. In this dimension the law concerned itself strictly with the exercise of private power. In battling for collective bargaining, what was permissible union conduct? But there was a second, more ambiguous dimension arising from what might be called the closed-shop paradox: Workers must be free before they can form unions, but the unions they form constrain their individual liberty. In America, where individual liberty weighed so heavily, labor law more than in any other country discounted the claims of solidarity in favor of the nonunion worker and, more to the point, the antiunion employer. Equally extraordinary was that this law was entirely the handiwork of judges. Not even Britain, in whose common law tracks the American courts followed, permitted the judiciary this kind of primacy.

The triumph of the American bench was double-edged. Its decisions were invested with the majesty of "found" law, but this law by the same token lacked any genuine democratic legitimization. Everything therefore depended on the courts' evenhandedness. The courts never found it within themselves, once the stakes began to rise after the Civil War, to be evenhanded, and the labor law they constructed unabashedly favored employers. The crisis of legitimacy was set finally into motion by *Hitchman v. Mitchell* (1917), which declared that unions, where yellow-dog contracts were in effect, could be enjoined from organizing because they were inducing breach of contract by the workers they were seeking to organize. As the meaning of *Hitchman* sank in and entire nonunion fields were walled off, revulsion against the courts became palpable. They had overreached themselves.

The upshot was the Norris-LaGuardia Act (1932), which declared the yellow-dog contract unenforceable in federal courts and effectively took from them the power to issue labor injunctions. After a century of acquiescence, Congress (and in its wake, key state legislatures) finally reined in the courts. There was nothing revolutionary, however, about what Congress intended. Norris-LaGuardia left the collective-bargaining struggle in the private sphere, where it had always been.

With the Wagner Act three years later, American labor law did break with its past. For one thing, the Section 7 principles of freedom of association became rights protected from employer coercion. This development, in truth, had been long in the making and in some form was probably inevitable after Norris-LaGuardia. What was unexpected, with no precedent behind it, was a state-mandated process for setting collective bargaining in motion. Union recognition would no longer be determined by equations of power but by a rule of law, which consisted of the provisions by which, on a showing of majority support in an appropriate unit, unions would be certified as exclusive agents with whom the employer was obliged to bargain. This privileged status, however, came at a price. The Wagner Act, in effect, translated the Section 7 right of employees "to bargain collectively through representatives of their own choosing" into an NLRB-supervised vote by workers, that is, into the exercise of an *individual* right.

Enemies of collective bargaining were quick to spy this chink in the armor of solidarity, and with the Taft-Hartley amendments of 1947 they pried it open, beginning symbolically with the insertion in Section 7 of the worker's right "to refrain from any and all [concerted] activities." From this language followed the right-to-work amendment—14(b)—inviting states to exempt themselves from the union-shop provision in the law. All this was preliminary to the main event, which was to expunge every vestige of self-organization from the process of determining representation. The aim was to restore "the American workingman['s] dignity as an individual." Antiunion employers now fight their battles at the NLRB ballot box, but they have been re-armed, as in pre–New Deal days, to weigh in as champions of free choice and individual rights, which is, of course, how *Avondale* presents itself.

But without the power to coerce, antiunion employers would have had a harder time of it. From the outset, the legal restraints on them had been limited—nothing more, on a finding of an unfair labor practice, than cease-and-desist orders. The test of any law, of course, is its capacity to command consent, and by that measure the Wagner Act was initially impressive. But resourceful employers soon realized that the NLRB could be resisted and ultimately stymied.

Why had the Wagner Act opted for unfair labor practices? The term itself, an adaptation of the Federal Trade Commission's unfair trade practices, was a product of the early New Deal's struggle to stabilize the industrial economy via the National Recovery Administration and its codes of fair competition. Everything in that corporatist experiment had to do with bureaucratic regulation, and so, it followed, did the emerging conception of labor's rights. Indeed, the Wagner Act's NLRB, with its quasi-judicial powers, seemed a bold advance by those who had known only the failed NRA labor boards. New Dealers, moreover, were great champions of an administrative state. The NLRB was a prideful example and was on that score, as a power unto itself, bitterly attacked by conservatives. We can catch the drift of contemporary progressive thinking by a Brookings study, which, responding to conservative criticism, concluded that "transportation, communication, shipping, public waters, labor relations, and the like" are properly the subject of the administrative process.[2] Note, of course, the submersion of labor's rights in this regulatory pool. But, in truth, the Brookings study had a point.

The Wagner Act really created a basket of rights, some of which, involving the duty to bargain, for example, or company domination of a labor organization, are perhaps best enforced—to use the Brookings' language—by "consistent, flexible, informed, intelligent, and developing administration." On workers' core right—not to be discriminated against or fired for union activity—no such claim could be made. Reducing this right to an unfair labor practice is explainable mainly by reference to a little-noticed truth about the Wagner Act: it had to be reconciled with a century of prior labor law and precedent.

The Supreme Court had already spoken definitively on the right to organize. The lead case was *Adair v. U.S.* (1908), striking down a provision of the Erdman Act (1898) that prohibited railroads from discharging workers for union membership. Inasmuch as the worker had an absolute right to quit, declared *Adair*, so had the employer an absolute right to fire him or her. "Any legislation that disturbs that equality is an arbitrary interference with liberty of contract."

In light of *Adair*, Norris-LaGuardia dealt with the yellow-dog contract and labor injunction procedurally and not, as the AFL would have preferred, on any claim of labor's inalienable rights. The Wagner Act, however, required a different maneuver inasmuch as it directly contravened *Adair*. The solution was supplied by Oliver Wendell Holmes, who in his dissent to *Adair* had argued that the employer's liberty was not being fundamentally challenged. Protecting union workers from discrimination was "in substance, a very limited interference with freedom of contract, no more." The Wagner Act eased into that accommodation by bundling this "very limited interference" with the lesser unfair labor practices, which opened the path by which the Supreme Court threaded its way past *Adair*.

The *Jones and Laughlin* decision upholding the Wagner Act declined to offer any substantive explanation, citing instead a 1930 decision involving the Railway Labor Act that turned on company domination of a labor organization, not the right to organize. The paragraph pronouncing *Adair* "inapplicable" is most notable, in fact, for the Court's anxiety to align the Wagner Act with liberty of contract and individual rights. It is in this context, in which the new law does not reverse, but accommodates itself to, established law that the weakness of labor's rights is to be understood. Unfair labor practices are themselves part of the accommodation.

So, where does this excursion into the law's origins leave us? One could argue that the labor movement might have been better off had history stopped with Norris-LaGuardia. But there is no way to retrace our steps to that juncture, when trade unions had been substantially empowered but remained free to fight their own battles. Where we can begin is with the conception of labor's rights that existed before anyone had thought of state-certified bargaining agents. This means disaggregating from the bundle of rights linked to representation the right to organize, which was, in point of fact, where a national consensus originally developed for our modern labor law.

That consensus still exists. Is there a politician or company president in this country prepared to stand up and defend the discharge of workers for joining a union? And it would be interesting, once labor got the country's attention, to hear the argument that injury to workers discriminated against for union membership is less than injury to workers discriminated against because of racial or sexual prejudice and less worthy of equal remedies. The main thing is to get the country's attention. The AFL-CIO is not lacking the means, providing it focuses its message, to place this issue on the national agenda. A first step might be to establish a well-publicized defense fund specifically dedicated to workers victimized because of their union activities.

The merits of this historically informed strategy are, first of all, practical. A right-to-organize campaign, more than any other lobbying battle the AFL-CIO might undertake, can be won and would, moreover, have immediate and real benefits out in the field. Second, because it invokes the most *individual* of labor's rights (in the sense that only individuals exercise the right and suffer the consequences), the right-to-organize issue will hit antiunion ideologues where it hurts most and align the labor movement with the individual-rights bent of the labor law, which, like it or not, seems to me not reversible.

From this, over the longer term, further reform might follow, most particularly reform of the representation election. The problem with the election is that it gives employers a platform for coercing workers. Taft-Hartley enabled this perversion of industrial democracy to happen, but the deed itself was done afterward—shades of labor's judge-ridden past!—by the post–New Deal NLRBs and the courts, whose charge it was to fashion a case law based on the Taft-Hartley revisions squaring the workers' right of free choice with employer "free speech" and property rights. What gives this case law its astounding prejudicial bent is the presumption, subterranean but ever-present, that workers' rights count for less than employers' rights. The electoral coercion arising from Taft-Hartley can be alleviated, perhaps even reversed, by a rebalancing of conflicting rights, with the right to organize as labor's lever, not to speak, of course, of eliminating the employer's most potent weapon in the election campaign: the discharge of his critics.

And, finally, some unions are voting with their feet on labor law. They are organizing workers directly, putting economic pressure on employers, and demanding voluntary recognition or neutrality pledges. In effect, they are trying to break the grip that NLRB certification currently holds on workers' access to collective bargaining. The right to organize, more spaciously conceived, would resist being confined, or given expression, only in the NLRB certification process. And we would be a step closer to the more open and diverse bargaining order the labor movement is groping toward.

This essay originally appeared in *New Labor Forum* (Fall–Winter 1998): 129–137. Used with permission.

Notes

1. The case was ultimately settled when Avondale was sold to new owners who were willing to deal with the union.
2. Frederick F. Blachly and Miriam E. Oatman, *Federal Regulatory Action and Control* (1940), quoted in Irving Bernstein, *The New Deal Collective Bargaining Policy* (Berkeley, 1950), 142.

Labor Rights as Human Rights: A Reality Check

There is an old saying about not looking gift horses in the mouth. The Human Rights Watch report on labor rights in America is truly a gift to all those working people struggling for, and being denied, full freedom of association.[1] The United States lectures the world about human rights, not least about the sanctity of freedom of association, yet its own practices fall sadly short of the international norms it champions. Insofar as Human Rights Watch instills the shame that might spark labor law reform, the report performs a great service. But the fact that labor people will find so much to agree with does not mean they should read into it virtues it does not have. They should not fail, so to speak, to inspect the teeth of this admirable gift horse.

The report meticulously describes American labor law as it currently operates and is exact in specifying how it should be altered to conform to international standards. It is written in a hallowed intellectual vein that the philosopher Morton G. White once called "formalism," in which the argument moves from first principles to prescribed actions. My skepticism really recapitulates the objection of progressives a century ago (including those illustrious founders of modern industrial relations, the Webbs and John R. Commons) that first principles are not a good guide to action.

Consider the selection of certified bargaining agents, which American labor law mandates be done by secret ballot. Some unions are turning against the representation election, preferring instead recognition strategies that shield workers from employer pressure. The report's author, Lance Compa, is not inclined to explore the merits of this development. He is satisfied that "a human rights analysis" can produce the correct remedy: "Human Rights Watch advocates more free speech for workers, not less free speech for employers."

Let me suggest what is problematic about this principled statement. First, it posits a false equality: Employer speech is the more powerful and is inherently coercive. This is not an original thought. The Wagner Act's authors understood it all too well and did their best to have employers barred from the unionizing process—that, in fact, was the original policy of the National Labor Relations Board. Second, the statement is insensitive about the ways in which representation elections go against the grain of American trade unionism as a movement-building institution. Organizers in the field know what they are up against. Viable organization comes after the election, not before; the tempo is dictated by the calendar of an administrative/judicial proceeding, one all too readily manipulated and drawn out by employers; and the drain on union resources can be enormous. That a formally democratic process might actually be harmful to freedom of association seems to fall below the screen of "human rights analysis."

Even viewed strictly as a rights question, the representation election involves besetting cross currents. The representation election is in the law as part of a grand transaction. The unions accepted a certification procedure alien to their voluntaristic traditions in exchange for state-mandated collective bargaining that would force recalcitrant employers to the bargaining table. But the employer's duty to bargain in American labor law is trumped by his liberty of contract, which is why, despite the best efforts of the NLRB, a third of all newly certified unions today never win first contracts and why, on top of everything else, workers are turning against the representation election.

This rights conflict, of course, is there for all to see. As the report itself notes, free collective bargaining is a "paramount principle" against which its proposed remedy for freshly certified unions—first-contract arbitration when employers obstruct an agreement—would have to be considered "extraordinary." What I want to argue, however, is that this visible conflict is only a manifestation of the true bent of American labor law, making it probably irreconcilable with international norms as Human Rights Watch understands them. Getting at that embedded truth requires an excursion into the law's history, about which, I have to say, the author, Lance Compa, is incurious. Otherwise he would never have chosen, as he explicitly does, to exclude from his discussion the right of individual workers not to associate.

Underlying this right is a principle—free labor, defined as the worker's absolute freedom to leave a job—so paramount as to be constitutionally enshrined in the Thirteenth Amendment, which prohibited not only slavery but also involuntary servitude. Liberty of contract in employment came to rest on the at-will doctrine that was a corollary of this triumph of free labor. It was in defense of liberty of contract, so understood, that *Adair v. U.S.* (1908) declared it unconstitutional for a federal law to prohibit railroads from firing workers for union membership.

In his dissent, Justice Holmes offered no principled counterstroke but only a plea for a minor exception protecting the right to organize justified on grounds of public policy and within Congress's authority to make. Holmes's dissent is the template for the legal strategy by which the Wagner Act got past *Adair* (which remains to this day authoritative on at-will doctrine). Although freedom of association is framed there in the language of rights, enforcing those rights derives only from the assertion of policy in the law that collective bargaining is to be encouraged. The beginning point for understanding American labor law is that it does not, and never did, rise to the principled level contemplated by human rights advocates today.

What level it might achieve was, of course, fiercely contested. The fact that the Wagner Act's passage in 1935 coincided with a great unionizing movement enabled it to function initially as a facilitator of "self-organization"—the first, as it happens, of labor's enumerated rights in the law. But once the organizing drives subsided, that progressive conception of the law foundered. Antiunion employers made an emboldening discovery: The NLRB could be resisted and, in the South, even intimidated. They were unerring about how the law could be ideologically turned—hence the Taft-Hartley language affirming the worker's right "to refrain from any and all [concerted] activities"—and unerring as well at identifying its core vulnerability.

This was the representation election, whose presence in the law was deeply at odds with Wagner's conception of freedom of association as a process of self-organization. What the law means today is the product of half a century of case law balancing "free choice" by workers against the free speech and property rights of employers. The "unfair advantage" that Human Rights Watch finds so at odds with international norms—interrogations, captive-audience meetings, the exclusion of organizers from company property, and intimidating speech—all arise from a weighing of rival rights, case by case, by the NLRB and the courts over many decades. The outcome, grotesque though it be, is not in the least arbitrary. It arises out of American judicial process in all its majesty and expresses the true hierarchy of rights in American law.

Equally intractable is the American violation that Human Rights Watch regards as most flagrant—the denial of the right of every worker to freedom of association. The United States claims that it meets that standard. The fact that some workers are not covered by the federal law "means only that they do not have access to the specific provisions of the National Labor Relations Act . . . for enforcing their rights to organize and bargain collectively." Although Compa scoffs at this State Department statement (the "only" in it means that the rights of uncovered workers "can be violated with impunity") it in fact accurately renders the unimpeachable view in American law that freedom of association exists, and the constitutional requirement is met, when it is not impeded by the state. In our statutory history, as I have said, protection from employer interference has been granted not as a matter of right but of public policy, doled out piecemeal, initially only to railroad workers and then, in the Wagner Act, excluding agricultural, domestic, and family-employed workers. Agricultural workers lost out mainly because of Senator Wagner's political calculation that his bill needed southern Democratic support. Equally pragmatic was the treatment of supervisory employees who were originally covered and then, under Taft-Hartley, excluded. This was because employers convinced Congress that the unionization of foremen was fatally eroding managerial control over the shop floor.

The fraught question of striker replacements turns out also to have been originally a coverage issue. The right of the employer to hire and (if he beat the union) retain strikebreakers was longstanding and not challenged by the drafters of the Wagner Act. The only question was whether strikebreakers would be defined as employees for purposes of the law. In the terms on which the debate was framed, Human Rights Watch would logically have sided with the strikebreakers because its position is that the rights of every worker deserve protection. That was, indeed, the argument made at the time by employers. In deciding, after some debate, for the inclusion of strikebreakers, the authors of the Wagner Act had a different consideration in mind. They were anxious that the new law not be seen as interfering with the status quo as regarded collective bargaining. Thereafter, striker replacement was uncontroversial, so much so that the ruling case, *NLRB v. Mackay* (1938), disposed of it by obiter dictum. If the issue is no longer about coverage, it still resides in the realm of pragmatic judgment. Saying that human rights are at stake doesn't hurt, but the compelling question, at least in the American experience, is more mundanely whether striker replacement impedes free collective bargaining, which, under current conditions, most certainly it does.

In 1998, Lance Compa tells us, the German firm Continental AG permanently replaced 1,450 strikers at its North Carolina tire plant. Asked how he could justify tactics he would not dream of using at home, the chief executive replied, in effect, this is America, not Germany. The labor movement will do better minding this global businessman than Human Rights Watch. Yes, insofar as its findings shame Americans, that is to the good. And in this globalizing era the international obligations the United States undertakes can begin to matter.[2] Beyond that, American unionists are on their own. "Human rights analysis" should not deflect them from the hard thinking it will take to negotiate a way through, or around, a legal system that, at its core, is not favorably disposed to the collective activity of workers. To put a gloss on our German CEO's observation: This is America, not the world.

Postscript: In its Voice@Work campaign, the AFL-CIO adopted the Human Rights Watch report and is arguing that American labor law is in violation of international human rights standards.

This essay originally appeared in the *British Journal of Industrial Relations* 39 (Dec. 2001): 601–5, and is reprinted with permission of Blackwell Publishing Ltd.

Notes

1. Lance Compa, *Unfair Advantage: Workers' Freedom of Association in the United States under International Human Rights Standards* (Washington, D.C., 2000).
2. Compa reports some glacial recent movement. Also noteworthy is the citation of international norms by the Supreme Court in *Lawrence v. Texas* (2003), striking down Texas's state sodomy law.

Rescuing Self-Organization

The National Labor Relations Act, whose stated purpose and original effect was to encourage collective bargaining, has been hijacked by its natural enemies. The law serves today as a bulwark of the "union-free environment" that describes nine-tenths of our private-sector economy. My aim is to identify the central process at work in this amazing outcome and, on that basis, suggest a course of action.

The core of the law, as true today as on the day FDR signed it in 1935, are three interlocking sections. Section 7 declares the rights of workers. These were not new in 1935. They had already appeared in the Norris-LaGuardia Anti-Injunction Act of 1932 and had been a long time evolving. Section 8 listed a set of unfair labor practices, acts that violated the Section 7 rights, which, under Section 10, the National Labor Relations Board was empowered to prevent. This was new but not surprising. The rights enunciated as public policy in Norris-LaGuardia were merely expressions of principle until the labor law made them enforceable. Sections 7 and 8 were reported out of Senator Wagner's committee as a package. Finally, Section 9 dealt with the issue of union recognition, setting forth the criteria that justified, in effect, a constraint on the employer's liberty of contract. It became an unfair labor practice to refuse to bargain, and bargain exclusively, with a labor organization chosen by a majority of the employees in an appropriate unit. Section 9 further provided that if the demonstration of majority support was supervised by the NLRB, the labor organization so chosen would be certified and officially designed as bargaining agent. For that purpose the NLRB could hold a secret ballot. It is this final wrinkle, the representation election, that is the focal point of my discussion. I want to defer any consideration of the defects that make unions increasingly hostile to the representation election and cut at once to what, viewed historically, is the crux of the problem, namely, that the representation election is the instrument by which labor's enemies have hijacked the law.

Historically, it was self-organization—workers freely associating to advance their common interests—that produced the labor movement and gave it legitimacy. Indeed, the definitive case establishing the legality of unions, *Commonwealth v. Hunt* (1842), grounded that finding on the view that trade unions were voluntary associations and presumed, in an enterprising society whose hallmark was voluntary association, to be in the public interest until, by the standards that applied to all combinations, they acted unlawfully. Trade unions embraced self-organization (and in Gompers' time elevated it, under the rubric of voluntarism, into the defining principle of the AFL), and so did the Wagner Act, whose enumeration of the rights of workers in Section 7 begins with self-organization. The succeeding rights (to assist, form, or join labor organizations, to bargain collectively, and to engage in concerted activity) all march in concert with self-organization—except in one respect. The right to bargain collectively is qualified by the words "through representatives of their own choosing."

This familiar phrase might seem unproblematic, inherent in any statement of worker rights, but, in fact, "representatives of their own choosing" has its own particular history. It first appeared, as best I can determine, during the labor crisis after World War I and was fashioned against a specific challenge: company unions—employee representation plans, so called—that gave employers the excuse that they need not deal with outside unions because their employees already exercised their right to organize and bargain collectively. The issue crystalized during the steel strike of 1919, the greatest recognition strike in American history. The union response was, okay, let the employees choose—and that's the origin of "representatives of their own choosing."

Nothing came of this effort; the steel strike, in a long train of failed recognition strikes, failed. But the issue had been injected into a grand conclave on a postwar labor policy for the nation and given a standing it might otherwise not have had. Once enunciated, employee choice stuck, finding its way into every subsequent federal law involving labor's rights, even the antiunion Transportation Act (1920) restoring the railroads to private ownership after the war.

Insofar as it targeted employer interference, of course, employee choice was consonant with self-organization, and that bent developed robustly in railway labor policy of the Hoover era, culminating with *Texas and New Orleans v. Railway Clerks* (1930), which upheld the disestablishment of a company union as a violation of the provision of the Railway Labor Act of 1926 prohibiting "interference, influence or coercion" by employers in the designation of representatives by employees. Company domination of a labor organization—a concept original to, and shining ornament of, the American labor law—begins here.

But implicit in "representatives of their own choosing" was also a procedural question, How was the will of workers to be revealed? And that produced the representation election. Unlike company-domination doctrine, however, not right away. This was because on the railroads, where the battle was originally confined, unions were well established, and choosing bargaining agents was not a salient issue. The Railway Labor

Act left it to "the respective parties"—one being the unions—to designate representatives.

Once the New Deal swept into power in 1933 and the battleground shifted to the unorganized mass-production sector, how the will of workers was to be revealed became very salient indeed. Employers immediately resurrected the company union, and almost overnight American industry was blanketed by employee representation plans. The conflict over freedom of choice that had been scrubbed in 1919 was now joined.

Forces bigger than the company union battle, of course, were also at work. One was the Great Depression itself, without which no Congress was likely to have overridden hallowed notions of liberty of contract and passed a law ordering employers to engage in collective bargaining. Another was the destabilizing effects of the mass-production revolution, without which the craft-oriented AFL was unlikely to have lost its grip on union jurisdiction—a central attribute of self-organization—and ceded oversight of appropriate bargaining units to the NLRB. But on the core issue, company unionism, it was the recently minted principle of "representatives of their own choosing" that was determining, so much so as to have produced in the final bill a kind of legislative overkill. This was because the drafters had been as intent on enforcing the anticompany-domination side of "representatives of their own choosing" as, on a parallel track, they were intent on devising the procedures for registering the will of the majority. The result was that for its intended function—to give workers a choice between company and independent unions—the representation election was instantly irrelevant. As company-dominated labor organizations, the employee representation plans were mostly barred from the ballot.

It didn't matter. The representation election, once in, was in. The democratic resonance was too great. Wagner, indeed, exploited it in just that way, pumping up the industrial democracy rhetoric on behalf of his bill to great effect. But the authors of the Wagner Act were not deceived. They knew that problems had been created for self-organization and, with great prescience, that self-organization and employer coercion were inversely related. Insofar as the boundaries of self-organization contracted, the scope for employer coercion expanded. Reading the legislative history of the Wagner Act with that issue in mind is one of the more interesting features of this exercise. Thus, to take a point that resonates today, Wagner's rejection of the charge that it was one-sided for employers and not unions to be guilty of unfair labor practices. This was a false equation, said Wagner. The purpose of the law was not to regulate self-organization.

There were plenty of laws protecting nonunion workers from physical intimidation or slashed tires, but only his law protected workers from economic coercion, and economic coercion was strictly the employer's weapon. Similarly, he argued that employers should be neutral during representation campaigns because anything they said was inherently coercive (and because they had no more legitimate interest when workers organized than did workers when employers organized). As for the election, it was not mandatory—the NLRB could use "any other suitable method"—underscoring that the process was in service to the self-organization of workers, which, in a time of massive CIO organizing, indeed it was. In the early years, NLRB certifications mainly ratified facts on the ground.

But not for long. With Taft-Hartley in 1947 the election became mandatory for certification. The "free-speech" right of employers to participate was affirmed, as was their right to petition for elections. Unions became subject, like employers, to unfair labor practices. The doctrinal underpinnings of this transformation are to be found in a new Section 7 right of employees not to participate in concerted activities, a principle made manifest specifically in the right-to-work 14(b) provision. Section 14(b) served as much to trumpet the individual rights reorientation of the law as to enable states to outlaw the union shop. The collective bargaining scheme was itself left intact—a nice final touch ensuring the future of the representation election that now stood at the core of that scheme. We should pause here to admire the unerring aim of the law's enemies. It would make an interesting research project to find out whether union people, for all their protests about a slave labor law, actually understood what was happening. I doubt it.

Senator Wagner had known that the erosion of self-organization meant exposing workers to employer coercion. His bad dreams have been far outdistanced by the current reality, which is that an employer with enough money and stomach for it can be confident of defeating any union challenge utilizing NLRB procedures. In the Clinton era, NLRB elections produced collective-bargaining rights for about seventy-five thousand workers a year. With the union attrition rate at a half million a year, we have a recipe for the virtual disappearance of private-sector unionism, provided that all organizing is channeled into NLRB elections. And that brings us to the endgame.

Elections are not the only route to collective-bargaining rights. The employer's duty to bargain (Section 8a[5]) is subject not to Section 9(c), which deals with elections, but to Section 9(a), whose operative words "designated or selected" unarguably mean more than elections.[1] This, of course, is another, and surely the most important, of Wagner's efforts at bolstering self-organization. Indeed, as the law is written, an employer is free to accept a union's claim of majority support and forego the Section 9(c) procedure. One can well imagine countries (as, for example, currently in the United Kingdom) where under such a scheme employers would routinely opt for voluntary recognition. Not in the United States. Here, voluntary recognition is itself a battleground, turning on this issue: Does the employer have an obligation to accept a union's claim of majority support? Yes, the case law originally said, a view codified in *Joy Silk* (1949) to mean the employer had a duty to bargain unless he could show "good faith doubt" about the authorization cards or other evidence of support. In 1966 the burden shifted to the union, which had to demonstrate a "course of conduct" of employer bad faith (*Aaron Brothers* [1966]). In the end, the employer was absolved of any duty to bargain without a representation election (*Linden Lumber* [1974]), providing he did not engage in unfair labor practices too egregious to permit an election. But unions can still pressure an employer to do what the law authorizes, hence the corporate campaigns that now accompany demands for card-check agreements. In recent congressional hearings, employers have railed against corporate campaigns, but they have limited legal recourse against what is essentially a free-speech activity.

So we have in 2002 the Norwood bill (H.R 4636) that proposes to outlaw card-check recognition and finish the job against self-organization. Do employers understand this? Listen to the spokesman for the Labor Policy Association that sponsored the Norwood bill. The trouble with authorization cards, he says, is that they "are signed in the presence of an interested party—a pro-union co-worker or an outside union organizer—with no governmental supervision."[2] The issue is not that unions coerce workers; that is already prohibited by Taft-Hartley. The issue is that workers talk among themselves and with organizers without "governmental supervision." That's how far we've come from Senator Wagner's celebration of self-organization.

The striking feature about the law's evolution is its sheer inexorability. Taft-Hartley was a turning point, yes, but in key ways it merely ratified or completed a case law already assaulting Wagner's defenses of self-organization. And, with virtually no further legislation, the work of interpreting labor's rights out of existence has steadily proceeded. The incremental dismantling of the duty to bargain can be replicated many times over in the case law governing interrogations, captive audience meetings, union access, and coercive speech—you name it.

One might argue that all this reflects is the political dispensation of post–New Deal America. Certainly, the law would have evolved more benignly had the New Deal coalition not foundered after World War II. It mattered, James A. Gross tells us in his exhaustive history of the NLRB, which party was in power. Yet the tendency of the case law, despite this ebb and flow, was irreversibly in one direction. This suggests that, beyond politics, deep-seated ideo-legal biases are built into the law's development.

It's actually hard to put a name to the Section 7 rights, but we can know what they are not by reference to one unfair labor practice with a different provenance, that is, not grounded in Section 7. This is the secondary boycott prohibition added by Taft-Hartley, for which there is a separate enforcement section (303) declaring this particular unfair labor practice by unions "unlawful" and enabling any person injured thereby in his business or property to sue in court for damages and legal costs. Why is it that the injury suffered by a worker discharged from her job for union activity does not call for equally robust redress, or the priority and immediate injunctive relief that the NLRB is directed to provide to employers in the case of secondary boycotts? Section 7 rights are weak rights, trumped every step of the way by property rights, by employer free speech, and by liberty of contract. And while this hierarchy of rights is broadly felt in the law's devolution, it is imprinted, most importantly, on the case law governing free choice. Indeed, if in one dimension the representation election fixes the individual worker into place so that he or she can be efficiently coerced, in another dimension it fixes the unequal contest of rights into place so that the courts can efficiently legitimize those necessary powers of employer coercion.

By now that string has about run out, and little is left to a liberal board, like Bill Clinton's, but administrative refinements. If the reader is interested in watching the unequal contest of rights in action, however, I have a suggestion. Think about where the labor law is still in play. Right. It's the corporate campaign. One potent weapon available to targeted employers are lawsuits that tie up the union and bleed its resources. But if the NLRB finds the lawsuit to be retaliatory, that's an unfair labor practice, and the employer can be enjoined and ordered to pay the union's legal costs. So now a heavyweight employer right is being wheeled out— the right of petition in the First Amendment, which, Justice Scalia suggests, is infringed if the employer is unduly discouraged from going to court.[3] Only a determined optimist would want to bet on the long-term future of NLRB doctrine on the retaliatory lawsuit.

How, I'm thinking, given the heavy hand of history, are we to make our way back to a labor law that fosters self-organization? Logic might say to attack the representation election. But, at the moment, that battle can't be won. The representation election is not going away. What we need is an issue that shifts the debate back to self-organization. In my view that's the right to organize, in the specific sense of the individual right of workers to associate. What is wanted is simple enough: penalties that actually deter employers and enable workers to organize without fear. Back pay and rehire, years later in discharge cases, manifestly do not deter employers. We should not underestimate the rejuvenating effect on union campaigns. Moreover, the right to organize is exercised by individuals and calls forth no rival employer rights. On both counts it is the most unassailable of labor's rights. Above all, a robust right to organize will revive the law's embrace of self-organization. Tactically, the crucial thing is to avoid making the right to organize part of an omnibus reform. The issue has to stand alone, where it cannot be obfuscated by talk about democratic elections and individual rights.

Labor can win a debate on the right to organize, but until another New Deal era comes along that's the only ideological debate it can. The AFL-CIO will do better when it does turn to omnibus reform, arguing that the law is outmoded; key features—the certification structure, employee definitions, and mandatory bargaining issues—rest on assumptions specific to a passing stage in our industrial development. This road leads, ultimately, to labor's liberation from the representation election. A long-term campaign might be called "A Labor Law for the Twenty-first Century."

At the moment, however, even the short term is beyond Washington. So we have to think about the states. This, of course, immediately invokes admonitions about preemption—the elaborately developed case law guarding federal regulation of labor relations against state interference. Union-side lawyers advise that any state action touching preemption is ill-advised because only adverse decisions are to be anticipated. The lawyers could be wrong; a skillfully crafted right-to-organize law might get by preemption.[4]

But for argument's sake, let's say the lawyers are right. The labor movement will want to weigh their caution against the opportunity costs of inaction. Consider instead a bold idea—a ballot proposition in a liberal state like California or Wisconsin for a constitutional amendment affirming freedom of association, with a proviso on the right to organize. A bill in the legislature might accomplish the same thing but wouldn't generate the public exposure that's the point of this exercise. Opponents will say the state can't do that because it's preempted. Are Californians or Wisconsinites likely to be deterred from defending the rights of their fellow citizens—or spurred on—when the scandalous failure of the federal law is made clear to them? Let's say then that the courts strike down the state law. Is anything better calculated to light a fire in Washington once a national debate has begun on the right to organize? When it comes to the states, after all, the objective is not to mitigate preemption but to prompt federal action that renders preemption irrelevant.

The endgame over the labor law is in play. Without a countering right-to-organize campaign the Norwood bill will pass, maybe not in this congressional session or the next but ultimately it will pass. And then the representation election's stranglehold will be complete. Self-organization will have been expunged from the law.

———————

Postscript: After this article was completed, the AFL-CIO unveiled its response to the attack on card check recognition—a bill (the Employee Free Choice Act) introduced in the U.S. Senate by Edward Kennedy and in the House by George Miller that would substitute card check for elections except when a certified or recognized exclusive bargaining agent was being challenged. In addition, violations of workers' rights during organizing campaigns would be subject to greater penalties and mandatory injunctions, and arbitration and mediation would become available in first contract disputes.

This essay originally appeared as "Labor vs. the Law" in *New Labor Forum* 13 (Spring 2004): 9–16. Used with permission.

Notes

1. *NLRB v. Gissel* 395 U.S. 575 (1969).
2. Daniel V. Yeager, "Testimony before the Health, Education, Labor and Pensions Committee, U.S. Senate," June 20, 2002, 3.
3. *BK&E Construction v. NLRB,* 122 S.C. 2003 (2002). I am grateful to Paul More for calling this case to my attention.
4. See, for example, Michael H. Gottesman, "Rethinking Labor Law Preemption: State Laws Facilitating Unionization," *Yale Journal of Regulation* 7 (Summer 1990): 355–410.

INDEX

DAVID BRODY is professor emeritus of history at the University of California, Davis. He is the author of *Steelworkers in America: The Nonunion Era, Workers in Industrial America: Essays on the Twentieth-Century Struggle, In Labor's Cause: Main Themes on the History of American Workers,* and other books.

*The University of Illinois Press
is a founding member of the
Association of American University Presses.*

---

*Composed in 9.5/12.5 Trump Mediaeval
with Trump Mediaeval display
by Celia Shapland
for the University of Illinois Press
Manufactured by Maple-Vail Book Manufacturing Group*

*University of Illinois Press
1325 South Oak Street
Champaign, IL 61820-6903
www.press.uillinois.edu*